PATTERNS

PATTERNS

BUILDING BLOCKS OF EXPERIENCE

Marilyn Charles

THE ANALYTIC PRESS

2002   Hillsdale, NJ   London

Published by The Analytic Press, Inc., Publishers. Editorial Offices: 101 West Street, Hillsdale, NJ 07642. www.analyticpress.com

Designed and typeset by Compudesign, Charlottesville, VA.

The lines from "Planetarium," the lines from "Shooting Script," from *The Fact of a Doorframe: Poems Selected and New, 1950-1984* by Adrienne Rich. Copyright 1975, 1978 by W. W. Norton & Company, Inc. Copyright 1981 by Adrienne Rich. Used by permission of the author and W. W. Norton & Company, Inc. The lines from "Transcendental Etude," the lines from "Origins and History of Consciousness," the lines from "Sibling Mysteries," the lines from "Power," the lines from "Hunger," Poem XX of "Twenty-One Love Poems," from *The Dream of a Common Language: Poems 1974-1977* by Adrienne Rich. Copyright 1978 by W. W. Norton & Company, Inc. Used by permission of the author and W. W. Norton & Co., Inc. The lines from "Sleepwalking Next to Death" from *Time's Power: Poems 1985-1988* by Adrienne Rich. Used by permission of the author and W. W. Norton & Company, Inc. The lines from "For Memory," the lines from "A Vision," from *A Wild Patience Has Taken Me This Far: Poems 1978-1981* by Adrienne Rich. The lines from "Merced," the lines from "From a Survivor," from *Diving into the Wreck: Poems 1971-1972* by Adrienne Rich. Copyright 1973 by W. W. Norton & Company, Inc. Used by permission of the author and W. W. Norton & Company.

Specified lines from "Three Women: A Poem for Three Voices" from *Winter Trees* by Sylvia Plath. Copyright 1968 by Ted Hughes. Reprinted by permission of HarperCollins Publishers Inc. and Faber and Faber Ltd., Publishers.

Chapter 2 is a revised version of a paper published in *The Journal of Melanie Klein and Object Relations*, 17:367-388, 1999; chapter 3 is a revised version of a paper published in *The American Journal of Psychoanalysis*, 61:239-269, 2001; chapter 4 is a revised version of a paper published in *The Psychoanalytic Quarterly*, 70:387-416, 2001; and chapter 6 is a revised version of a paper published in *Psychoanalytic Psychology*, 18:340-364, 2001. Copyright 2001 by the Educational Publishing Foundation. Adapted with permission.

Library of Congress Cataloging-in-Publication Data
Charles, Marilyn
   Patterns : building blocks of experience / Marilyn Charles
     p. ; cm
   Includes bibliographical references and index
   ISBN 0-88163-372-0
   1. Psychoanalysis. 2. Perception. 3. Pattern perception. 4. Senses and sensation. I. Title.
   [DNLM: 1. Perception. 2. Creativeness. 3. Kinesics. 4. Self Concept. 5. Sensation. BF
   311 C476p 2002]
   RC506 .C485 2002
   616.89'17-dc21   2002074795

Printed in the United States of America

10   9   8   7   6   5   4   3   2   1

CONTENTS

FOREWORD

"In the beginning was the word" has long been a rallying cry, not only for evangelical Christianity, but also for psychoanalysis itself.

Although Freud early on spoke of "infantile sexuality" (1905) and the "infantile neurosis" (1915), he and his followers really believed that the origins of an infant's mental life began after the decline of primary narcissism as the oedipal phase was coming on line—to say nothing of the belief by most analysts today that psychoanalysis is the therapy of the word and that all experiences must ultimately be transformed into words if they are to achieve meaning. Until recently infant development research findings suggested that infants (actually toddlers) began mental life with the acquisition of speech (Stern, 1985). Current research findings suggest that an infant experiences some degree of separateness at birth and becomes emergent as a self and object-directed immediately (Beebe and Lachmann, 2002). Along this line, there has long existed a difficulty among psychoanalysts, particularly adult analysts, in reconciling the burgeoning data from infant development research with psychoanalytic reconstructions from adult analysis.

One of the difficulties in this regard was in establishing if and how infants could process their experiences from internal and external stimuli in the light of their utter immaturity to register feelings and to express themselves articulately. Gradually a school of psychoanalytic thought developed that propounded that infants were separate and individuated and related to objects from the very beginning. Melanie Klein, the founder of this school, extended Freud's concept of unconscious phantasy to the first year of life. Her ideas, however, were considered contentious and unprovable by most non-Kleinian analysts largely because the latter, along with infant developmentalists at the time, could not comprehend how infants could "think," let alone process, experiences without possessing verbal ability (Isaacs, 1952). The Kleinians believed that a preverbal (prelexical) infant was dominated by sensual imagery, a situation in which the representation of the object was identical with the object itself. Segal (1957) terms this phenomenon "symbolic equation." It is only with the attainment of the ability for verbalization that the infant, as toddler, could separate the representation from the object as a symbol to be thought about, she states. The consequence of this way of thinking was to grant that infants have a mind that could use a preverbal language to process their experiences and to convey them as affects to their objects by way of projective identification.

Gradually it has emerged from infant development research that infants possess a comparatively sophisticated preverbal information-processing capacity of their own (Beebe and Lachmann, 2002). Amodal and cross-modal capacities have been discovered whereby sensory information could be passed from one sense organ to another. Also brought to light is that infants experience affects and communicate them to their primary objects for processing, a feature that ultimately became known as the holding environment, the container and the contained, maternal reverie, bonding and attachment, and, more currently, affect attunement. Charles, supporting Klein's notions of early emergence of phantasies, believes that early phantasies arise in the context of early sensory experiences as nonverbal memories and become "remembered" as patterns of experience. In other words, Charles proffers the concept that pattern or shape constitutes the veritable container or enclosure of the affects and thereby gives them definition. She also believes that a rudimentary form of symbol manipulation, that is, thinking, occurs when sensory information is transferred from one modality to another.

Despite these findings from current infant development research, it is still difficult—partly because of the intricacies inherent in understanding how infants process their experiences, even with material assistance—for many psychoanalysts to conceive that preverbal infants can have a mental and social life, to say nothing of an unconscious mental life. Progress is being made, however. Recently, Johan Norman (2001), a Swedish child psychoanalyst, became an infant psychoanalyst by being able to reach, verbally, preverbal infants. His belief is that prelexical infants possess some capacity to understand carefully presented words from adults by being able to comprehend the prosody and affective intonations of the adult's speech. The conflict that we have long associated with the myth of the Tower of Babel has now come to pass. In all probability, infants possess a prelexical communicating system, one based on sensory imagery, of which phantasy is a subset, that may be destined either to disappear or to undergo primal repression with the onset of verbal acquisition.

Marilyn Charles's recent spate of writings explores this prelexical period and seeks to unravel its epistemological and communicative mysteries. She brings special tools for this task. Not only is she a practicing psychoanalyst, she is also a gifted poet and artist; and brings all three talents to bear in shedding light on how infants organize and communicate their experiences. She also seeks to integrate traditional and current psychoanalytic thinking with infant development research. Her reconciling and integrating instrument is her concept of patterns (or forms, contours, constellations), an idea that an artist would naturally consider. The appearance as well as the detection of these patterns is conducted by primary process. Earliest experiences, according to Charles, become integrated as patterns that ultimately devolve into meanings. Meaning and regulatory capacity become intertwined, she believes. In the beginning there is little if any difference between psychic and somatic distinctions in these patterns. Rhythmicity of sensations is experienced by infants as a soothing and predictable pattern. Charles further states, "nonverbal understandings are 'remembered' as patterns of experience."

Along a similar line, Anton Ehrenzweig (1967) states:

> [C]reative work succeeds in coordinating the results of
> unconscious undifferentiation and conscious differenti-
> ation and so reveals the hidden order in the unconscious.
> . . . In creativity, outer and inner reality will always be
> organized by the same indivisible process. . . . [T]he pri-
> mary process is a precision instrument for creative scan-
> ning that is far superior to discursive reason and logic.
>
> Piaget has given currency to the term "syncretistic"
> vision as the distinctive quality of children's vision and
> of child art. Syncretism[1] also involves the concept of
> undifferentiation. Around the eighth year of life a dras-
> tic change sets in in children's art. . . . While the infant
> experiments boldly with form and colour in represent-
> ing all sorts of objects, the older child begins to analyse
> these shapes by matching them against the art of the
> adult. . . . He usually finds his work deficient. . . . Much
> of the earlier vigour is lost. . . . What has happened is
> that the child's vision has ceased to be total and syn-
> cretistic and has become analytic instead [pp. 5–6].

For Charles, patterning constitutes a hidden order that may
be a subset of this syncretism that Ehrenzweig attributes to primary process. Similarly, I interpret Ehrenzweig as stating that
primary process is to be considered the hidden order of creativity and that it uses a syncretic field-scanning approach to
data gathering. Today we would attribute these processes to
right-cerebral hemispheric activity, and we now have reason to
believe that infants are right-hemisphere-dominant (Schore,
1994). It appears, then, that Ehrenzweig confirms Charles's
central theme.

---

1. The essence of "syncretism" here is that of scanning the whole,
undifferentiated field rather than focusing on individual details.

Bion (1959, 1962) substituted his own concept of "alpha function" for Freud's primary process and added aspects of secondary process to it.[2] Matte-Blanco (1975, 1988) takes up the issue of syncretism with his idea of symmetry. An infant's mind, according to him, is dominated in the main by symmetrical logic (primary process) rather than asymmetrical logic (secondary process). He also asserts that emotions are symmetrical.

If we put Piaget's and Ehrenzweig's concept of syncretism together with Freud's notion of primary process, Bion's concept of alpha function, Matte-Blanco's idea of symmetrical logic (actually, bilogic dominated by symmetry),[3] and Charles's artistic-esthetic notion of patterns, we have a unifying bridge that effectively links psychoanalytic theory and practice with infantile epistemology, ontology, phenomenology, and behavior. After reading Bion and then Charles, one might conceive of affects as impression-molds created on our sense organs by the impact of experience (what Bion, 1965, 1970, 1992, enigmatically called "O") of which we first become aware by being able to detect the emotional patterns these impressions have made on us. The patterns become the signature of the experience. Patterning is thus a basic and fundamental emotional data-processing system (prelexical) that anticipates a later cognitive system (lexical) for naming the emotions with words. Conversely, affects are patterned phenomena in self and others. We know ourselves and others by our patterns.

Charles expands on her basic theme of patterns by showing how they become the building blocks of our future identity. Her

2. Charles makes the interesting point that Bion's alpha function, in conjunction with its aim to detect the "selected fact," is a way of detecting patterns.

3. Actually, an infant, like the unconscious itself, is dominated by "bilogic," which is a binary opposition of symmetry and asymmetry in varying reciprocal proportions. The aliquot of symmetry for the infant would far exceed asymmetry, unlike for the adult, for whom the proportions would be reversed.

chapter on "Nonphysical Touch and Containment" deals with the clinical use of pattern detection of the analysand by the analyst. The use of patterns as an instrument of our creative potential comprises yet another chapter. Her final chapter, "The Language of the Body: Allusions to Self-Experience in Women's Poetry" is an in-depth study of several leading women poets and how their patterns of relationship to their bodies appear in their poetry.

This is not a work on esthetics so much as it is an esthetic work on psychoanalysis, one that adds dimension, clarity, and richness to it.

REFERENCES

Beebe, B. & Lachmann, F. M. (2002), *Infant Research and Adult Treatment: Co-Constructing Interactions.* Hillsdale, NJ: The Analytic Press.

Bion, W. R. (1959), Attacks on linking. In: *Second Thoughts.* London: Heinemann, 1967, pp. 93–109.

———— (1962), *Learning From Experience.* London: Heinemann.

———— (1965), *Transformations.* London: Heinemann.

———— (1970), *Attention and Interpretation.* London: Tavistock.

———— (1992), *Cogitations.* London: Karnac Books.

Ehrenzweig, A. (1967), *The Hidden Order of Art.* Berkeley: University of California Press.

Freud, S. (1905), Three essays on the theory of sexuality. *Standard Edition,* 7:125–245. London: Hogarth Press, 1953.

———— (1918), From the history of an infantile neurosis. *Standard Edition,* 17:3–122. London: Hogarth Press, 1955.

Isaacs, S. (1952), The nature and function of phantasy. In: *Developments in Psycho-Analysis* by M. Klein, P. Heimann, S. Isaacs & J. Riviere, ed. J. Riviere. London: Hogarth Press, pp. 67–121.

Matte-Blanco, I. (1975), *The Unconscious as Infinite Sets.* London: Duckworth Press.

———— (1988), *Thinking, Feeling, and Being: Clinical Reflections on the Fundamental Antinomy of Human Beings.* London: Tavistock/Routledge.

Norman, J. (2001), The psychoanalyst and the baby: A new look at work with infants. *Internat. J. Psychoanal.,* 82:83–100.

Schore, A. (1994), *Affect Regulation and the Origin of the Self: The Neurobiology of Emotional Development*. Hillsdale, NJ: Lawrence Erlbaum Associates.

Segal, H. (1957), Notes on symbol formation. *Internat. J. Psycho-Anal.*, 38:391–397.

JAMES S. GROTSTEIN

PROLOGUE

$\mathcal{W}$hen I was a child, I would "play" with patterns, creating objects from the evolving shapes in wood grains, marble, landscapes, and other patterned materials. As an analyst, I connect this way of entertaining myself with both creative and evasive forces, and recognize within this juncture a crucial fulcrum from which one might move forward or retreat further.

We can see disparate resolutions to this dilemma. Anne, for example, learned to avoid an overwhelmingly hostile and abusive childhood environment by entering into the landscape of the painting that hung in the family living room. In this way, she was able to effectively retreat from the extant reality into her created one, until she finally frightened herself back into the consensual world. We can contrast this path with that of Elena, who was able to create musical themes from the patterns she entered into as a respite from a critical and condemning object world, but was then caught by her inability to believe that same world could find value in her productions.

Pattern is a fundamental and essential aspect of being. It inheres in nature as well as in our experiences, which become patterned onto us as surely as the evolving lines of age upon the face. We can "see" these patterns through whatever modalities are most finely tuned in us. We create and re-create them through whatever means is at hand: in our relationships, our art, our work, our visions. Like earthworms, we eat our way through the universe, our "leavings" commingling with those of others, digesting and re-digesting via the unique instrument that is the self.

Our conceptions of "reality" are inevitably configured by the instruments through which we perceive. My childhood and young adulthood bridged an era in which changing conceptions of gender and gender roles offered new opportunities and new visions, constrained and molded by the previous generation's struggles for identity and self-definition. It is important for children to be able to identify with both same-sex and other-sex role models. The legacy of restrictive ideas about gender made it difficult, however, to identify with both parents without splitting into good versus bad, self versus other.

Cultural beliefs and family myths help to form our ideas about reality and also limit our ability to see beyond those myths. One of the myths in my family was that I looked "just like" my father, thereby excluding my mother, who was denied a part of her own legacy and value. Because of how meanings were assigned in my family, being "like" my father had more value. And so, I wanted to identify with my father, even though I was "like" my mother in ways that I valued highly. Identifying with my mother was hazardous in that she had not learned to value herself without great ambivalence. The hazard came in not wanting to be *de*valued in kind. Being like my mother became a treacherous path, on which one must always watch one's step lest one fall, along with her, into the mire. In this way, both identification and disidentification obscured and devalued the self, impeding self-acceptance, understanding, and growth.

My identity as an adult had been formed, in part, by disidentifying with the bad/devalued parts of my mother. This disidentification left the devalued, disowned aspects of self relatively inaccessible to working through. Coming to value those characteristics in my mother and in myself became an important facet of my own development.

Years later, as my mother was dying, I was better able to value her gifts and her legacy. In some ways, however, my understanding of our resemblance was superficial. Although I could "know" it in a rational sense, I was relatively unaware of its embodiment. Spending more time with her, and with the people who knew her well, reflected back to me fundamental aspects of my mother in myself. Gazing at my mother's face through the long days and nights of her illness, I began to see the strong similarities in the bones that structured our faces, as well as the gifts and values that structured our lives. I became strikingly aware of ways in which I carried her within me: in the turn of a phrase, the tilt of the head, the gesture of an arm or hand, an expression on my face. I became aware, at a whole new level, of having taken in my mother in myriad forms, and began to encounter her from the inside out, in my movements, my interactions, my thoughts and feelings.

In the months after her death, I have learned to love the memories of my mother that I carry within me in these nonverbal, unthought, profoundly meaningful patterned aspects of my being: from the ways in which I carry my body and inhabit the physical world, to the receptivity of my presence and the acuity of my understanding.

This book represents the fruits of my musings on how profoundly we become patterned by our experiences. It also represents an invitation to reap from that bounty by becoming more receptive to the incredible richness of these elemental units of meaning that may be quite idiosyncratic and yet are eminently comprehensible if we are willing to enter into the dance: to participate in them, to partake of them, and thereby to offer back to our patients an opportunity to break beyond the patterns that become an overlay—occluding meaning—to the underlying patterns that enhance understanding, thereby offering a means for richer, more adaptive living.

ACKNOWLEDGMENTS

A book is a tapestry, weaving together those threads that seem most crucial to the vision being put forward. The threads that have come together to make up this book are so various that it is difficult to gather them all in one small space without losing the richness, texture, and color.

In the interest of brevity, however, I will gather together a few major strands and thank collectively my friends and colleagues at the Michigan Psychoanalytic Council who have supported my work and provided a forum through which to begin the dialogue that resulted in this book. I acknowledge with deep appreciation the many editors and reviewers who have helped me clarify my thinking and writing over the years. They expanded this forum to include a wider group of colleagues and friends, providing an interchange that has been incredibly enriching. Most notably, I would like to thank Jim Grotstein, whose comments always lead me deeper into the labyrinth, and whose faith in my work has sustained my own. His unfailing support and clarity of vision have been like beacons, helping me to find my way in this journey of discovery. I am also grateful to the people at the Analytic Press who provided a home for me and for my work. To each of you I offer my sincere appreciation.

I feel profound gratitude to my friends and family, who have taught me so much about life and love. Memories built from these relationships have become a many textured fabric, informing my work and play. With deep appreciation, I dedicate this book to those who gave it life: my parents, sisters, husband, and children, who have brought me to the furthest recesses of joy and sorrow.

From the swirl of patterns that become what Bion called our "memories of the future," I have taken from my mother her acute aesthetic sense along with her incredible insight and courage; from my father his absolute integrity, endurance, and loyalty. From my sisters, I take friendship, in all its intricacies and potency. Assimilating these patterns of love and care helped me to find my husband, who has been all this and more, leaving it to my children to bring this dreamer more fully into the world, each bringing their own unique gift: through Devon I learned of joy and the pleasures of the interpersonal world; through Justin, faith and hope; through Jonathan, acceptance and determination.

Last, but never least, I offer my profound gratitude to all those individuals who have entrusted me with their histories and futures; trials and successes; dreams and visions. It is only through the gift of their trust that I have been able to engage with them in the extraordinary journey that becomes the road to greater self-understanding.

I

MEANING AND PRIMARY EXPERIENCE

*O*ur most essential understandings of self and world are based, not on rational logic, but rather on our deepest sense of what it means to be human. The analyst uses self-experience as the template on which self and other might be understood, through evolving variations on one's basic themes. Our primary "knowings" are experienced as "intuitions" that ground and guide us as we move through our lives. These intuitions have their foundations in our earliest experiences, which are primarily sensory, with little differentiation between self and other (Mancia, 1981). They are integrated as patterns that come to have meanings over time, whether or not we are conscious of them. These patterns reside in the domain of reverie: in those moments when we can still the voice of reason sufficiently to encounter our own basic truths.

The preverbal world is one of sensation, in which meanings accrue through the regularities and disregularities in our experience. As light and dark, heat and cold, comfort and discomfort, and other basic antitheses come to order sensory experience, the interactive rhythmicity of the sensations becomes the context within which the infant develops. Aspects of the mother's mental and emotional world are transmitted to the infant through many modalities, including hormonal and neuroendocrine means, the rhythmicity of heartbeat and blood pressure, the quality of voice, and the relative tension of the containing body. As development proceeds, bringing greater levels of complexity, rhythmicity and constancy become the essential principles by which the world is "decoded" (Mancia, 1981).

Early phantasies[1] are preverbal, configured by the sensory experiences that give rise to them (Isaacs, 1948). Words then provide a framework for organizing memories and sorting them in terms of categories, thereby facilitating their retrieval in verbal form. Overwhelming affect inhibits the capacity to organize experience, however, so that traumatic memories tend to be "encoded primarily at the sensory-motor level rather than in symbolic linguistic form" (Person and Klar, 1994, p. 1190). Nonverbal memories become stored within the body, leaving them relatively inaccessible to conscious awareness. Bodily memories may be expressed in numerous ways, including somatic distress or patterned movements. Although these types of "primitive communications" (McDougall, 1974) may be difficult to understand, they may also be extremely useful toward furthering our understanding of nonverbal memories and unconscious phantasies.

The biological and psychical become increasingly differentiated over time. Self-experience configures the templates on which meanings are understood and elaborated. Sameness and difference—comfort and discomfort—become the context within which self is differentiated from other and goals are established. Both symbol-formation and communication depend on the ability to transform sensory and affective experiences, in movements from primary process to the greater integration involved in secondary elaboration. This may make early and traumatic memories particularly inaccessible, unless we can interpret the primary "language" encoded within the body's rhythms. Becoming attentive to the variousness of signals of affective memory helps facil-

---

1. I am using the spelling "ph-" for unconscious phantasy and "f-" for conscious fantasy in accordance with the distinction articulated by Segal (1981).

itate greater conscious awareness and integration of primitive, disparate, or disowned experiences.

As the capacity for symbolic thought develops, there is a greater reliance on language, as more primary sensory aspects of knowing shift to the background and become, to some extent, disowned. However, nonverbal understandings are still "remembered" as patterns of experience, which are fundamental to our experiences of self, other, and world, whether or not they are accessible through the verbal mode. For example, we each respond to the word "mother" in terms of the mass of sensation, affective tone, imagery, and coloration that become the underpinnings of any verbal language that we might impose on them. These underpinnings are what Bion (1963) termed preconceptions, the basic sensory floor (Grotstein, 1985) upon which meanings are derived; what Bollas (1987) referred to as the "unthought known." The preconception is a basic sense of "how things are," derived from previous experience. Although we can use a given term to communicate with one another, as analysts we are always looking beyond the consensual meanings to these deeper layers: the more complex meanings and intonations underlying an individual's idiosyncratic use of a term.

THE INTERACTIVE CONTEXT

Nonverbal understandings have their foundations in interactions with caregivers, on whom the infant depends for the regulation of somatic and affective states. These early interactions not only prescribe the underlying sensory and affective meanings of being-with self and other, they also proscribe the capacity to engage and to assimilate. Sufficient responsiveness from caregivers, along with some nonresponsiveness, builds both safety and frustration tolerance, the rudiments of the child's own developing capacity for self-regulation (Fonagy and Target, 1997).

Meaning is created in and constrained by these early interactions, in the quality of the responsiveness between self and other. Regulatory capacity and meaning become inextricably intertwined, as the child's ability to take in new information is constrained by the capacity to regulate affect. When affect cannot be sufficiently regulated, it becomes an obstacle to well-being rather than being useful for its signal functions. At the extreme, exposure to overwhelming affect can be so traumatic that affect itself becomes a signal for evasive measures, such as splitting or defensive denial (Krystal, 1988). This contributes to the disowning of primary knowings, thereby impeding the ability to learn from experience and to make one's own way in the world.

Many people enter into therapy because of problems in affect regulation that impede self- and relational development. This capacity is then expanded within the containing environment of the therapeutic relationship through which the self can become known in relation to a responsive other. This relationship becomes the ground on which the work is built, derived within the evolving prosodies of self and other that come to form new templates for relationship. In reciprocal fashion, the greater capacity for relatedness that ensues becomes the context in which new meanings can be derived and built.

For our patients who have had little experience of a responsive other, establishing a relationship may be the most important part of the work. For some, such as Elena (described in chapter 5), there is a split between the grandiose self and the deprecated self that leaves them feeling doomed. Imperfection (humanness) becomes the essential flaw that erodes any developing sense of self-esteem. Our acceptance of the whole person becomes an invitation to know the self without defensive denial and attacks on understanding. This provides an opportunity to experience attunement in the context of an intimate relationship in a way that had been precluded by failures in the original parent–child dyads.

Early experiences of affective attunement—or resonance with a responsive other—form the basis of amodal experiences (Stern, 1985), in which information is translated from one sensory modality into another while preserving its essence. In amodal experiences, it is the basic underlying form or pattern that carries meaning, thereby expanding the potentialities for both self-regulation and interpersonal communication. This type

of communication entails the capacity to discriminate both sameness and difference as essential elements of meaning are transposed from one experience to another.

Infant research has affirmed what is most likely an inherent
ability to categorize across multiple domains, via distinct attributes of stimuli such as orientation, hue, angle, and form (Quinn,
1994). As infants develop, they become able to attend to, and
discriminate between, an ever wider range of perceptual fea-
tures (Cooper and Aslin, 1994) and become differentially
responsive to specific patternings, such as pitch contours
(Papousek et al., 1990; Fernald, 1993). We learn to process an
amazing array of perceptual stimuli and to derive meanings that
inform our understandings without necessarily being accessible
to conscious processing.

Amodal processing may be seen as a rudimentary form of
symbol manipulation, in which there is a displacement from one
sensory modality to another, a precursor for the capacity to transpose between mental modalities as well (Kumin, 1996). In this
way, categorical distinctions are made that are then used to make
finer discriminations in (and thereby make sense of) self and
environment. This differential responsiveness is diminished,
however, in the presence of strong affect.

The crucial ability to note sameness and difference formed
the basis for Matte-Blanco's (1975) theories about unconscious
processes. He posited two types of rules (that together form a
system of "bi-logic"): conscious (asymmetrical) logic and unconscious (symmetrical) logic. Whereas symmetrical logic grounds
us by noting similarities, it is through secondary process that we
make sense of our experience by establishing distinctions
between like things. Matte-Blanco conceptualized the unconscious in terms of overinclusive sets in which distinctions tend
to blur, resulting in such familiar phenomena as displacement,
condensation, and absence of negation. In the unconscious,
principles of generalization prevail to the point where like
becomes same. This process is termed "symmetrization" by Matte-
Blanco, in that the parts are seen as equal to the whole and similarity becomes equivalence.

Symmetrical logic tends to prevail in dreams and in those aspects of our daily lives more highly saturated by emotion or sensory experience. This tendency has important ramifications for memory, as intense affective experiences seem to be stored in such a way that any facet that has been linked to the experience can evoke a resurgence of the affect (Bucci, 1997a). Affective flooding inhibits the ability to process the material in verbal form, thereby tending to result in retraumatization rather than mastery. In this way, we can see that the caretaker's ability to moderate affect has vital implications for the child's ongoing capacity to be responsive to cues from both self and other, an essential condition for psychic growth (see Smith, 1990). In kind, the analyst's ability to provide an environment in which difficult material can be processed, rather than merely being recreated, becomes vital for psychic development.

IMPLICIT UNDERSTANDINGS

Many of our experiences are specifically understood through our experience of their pattern—or inherent order—beyond any capacity to consciously represent or name these patterns. Infant studies suggest that the more implicit dyadic intercommunications form the background for the slower—and more constrained—verbally encoded interactions. These implicit communications become the basis for understandings that have been termed variously "procedural knowledge" (Clyman, 1991; Fonagy, 1998) or "implicit relational knowing" (Stern et al., 1998), and may be best conceptualized in terms of a field theory, in which events are essentially and inherently interconnected (Kulka, 1997). Affect, for example, is to some extent separate from and prior to cognitive memory, thereby exerting an influence on secondary processes whether or not the affect becomes conscious (Krystal, 1988).

Stern (1985) described affect as "the supra-modal currency into which stimulation in any modality can be translated" (p. 53). Affective resonance occurs at a very basic primary sensory level and appears to be processed amodally. It is experienced in terms of both amplification of experience (intensity) and hedonic tone (pleasure vs. unpleasure) (Tomkins, 1982), and appears to be linked across multiple facets of experience (Bucci, 1997a). The basic pattern of the affect comes to carry meanings beyond the specific modality in which the information is conveyed. For example, Tomkins (1987) has described how "innate affect mechanisms structurally embody rules for differential resonance to every major *abstract* profile of neurons firing in terms of its level of change or its rate of change" (p. 148). Tomkins (1962) saw affect as essentially scripted in that, for example, a sudden increase of neural firing is linked to interest, startle, or fear; or to anger or distress if the stimulation is prolonged. The sudden reduction in positive affect associated with disrupted excitement or enjoyment, in contrast, tends to elicit shame.

We tend to think of affect in discrete, categorical terms. This framework diminishes our awareness of some of the more subtle aspects of affect that also come to carry meanings. Stern (1985) highlighted those aspects of affect that are not categorical, but rather are more dynamic and describe the contour of experience, as "fleeting," "decrescendo," or "explosive," for example. His use of the term "vitality affects" to characterize these contours is unfortunate in that this terminology appears to sever an aspect of affect and to reify it, giving the illusion of categorical distinctions to qualitative dimensions. His alternative term "activation contour" may be less subject to misinterpretation, pointing as it does to the form itself.

As Tomkins (1962) noted, affect is inherently a patterned phenomenon in terms of both our internal experience and our ability to perceive its traces on the visage of the other (Ekman, 1982) or in body position or gesture. Sensitivity to these patterns of interaction appears to be integrated far more rapidly than conscious, verbal awareness. Patterned experiences, such as rhythmicity and its disruptions, come to provide important cues as to one's relative safety and the likely trajectory of an interaction. Psychoanalysts' conjectures are based in part on sensations occasioned by interactions with the patient: with how they hold us in their world. Our resonance, or "countertransference," provides us with essential information at a very basic level. In this way, our experiences of attunement and misattunement afford important opportunities to better understand previous experiences, particularly those that may have occurred before the individual was old enough to build verbal memories.

MOVING TOWARD THE EXPLICIT

Over time, attempts to accommodate to disjunction through the use of symbolic functions bring greater control over self and environment. Real control diminishes the need to resort to omnipotent fantasies or other primitive defenses, such as splitting and defensive denial, that encourage a blurring of boundaries. These blurred boundaries may relieve anxiety, but do so at the price of psychic growth. In projective identification, for example, there is a lack of differentiation between self and other that obscures reality and constrains development.

Psychic growth is grounded in our actual experience. In this regard, the ability to distinguish between self and object, to note what Matte-Blanco (1975) has termed the "asymmetry" among like things, serves important developmental and integrative functions. As this capacity develops, "the symbol proper . . . is felt to represent the object; its own characteristics are recognized, respected, and used" (Segal, 1957, p. 395). This important developmental milestone is highlighted by Winnicott (1971) in his explication of the "use of the object." Our capacity to remain both connected and separate in this way offers an opportunity for consensual understanding: an integral aspect of the search for meaning. In this search, symbol formation provides a continuing dialectic in which internal and external realities can be integrated, whereby we "can be consciously aware and in control of symbolic expressions of the underlying primitive phantasies" (Segal, 1957, p. 396).

Just as symbol formation moves from the idiosyncratic toward the consensual, so too does the development of thought move from primary sensory experience toward the greater elaboration so important for interpersonal communication. Many

authors have attempted to describe this "sensory floor" of experience (Grotstein, 1985), the ground on which the experience
of self becomes elaborated. Ogden (1989), for example, posited
the "autistic-contiguous position" as a way of speaking about
these primary sensory modes of taking in and organizing experience. From this position comes the direct sensory experience
of basic forms or patterns that have fundamental "meanings"
(in the loosest sense of the word) in terms of basic bodily states
or stasis.

Although Ogden (1989) suggested adding this autistic-
contiguous position to those delineated previously by Klein, it
may be more usefully conceptualized as one pole of the paranoid-
schizoid position, moving along a continuum toward a greater
dimensionality, as experience builds on experience (Charles,
2001a). According to Klein (1957) and her followers, in the paranoid-schizoid position the basic form or sensation becomes more
richly elaborated yet remains essentially unlinked, fragmented.
It is then in the depressive position that the elaboration takes
on the dimensionality of perspective—what we most often term
"meaning," in the sense of "understanding" or "knowing-about."
This sequence would seem to move from an emphasis on primary to secondary process, from what Matte-Blanco (1975, 1988)
described as the symmetrical mode of being, into the realm of
disjunctions wherein elaborated meanings can be verbalized and
exchanged.

Ogden's (1989) autistic-contiguous position would seem to
roughly parallel what Matte-Blanco (1975) described as symmetrical being. As Matte-Blanco (1975) suggested: "the sensation is, in itself, a primary experience, which is irreducible to
description, though we constantly try to describe it. The same
is true of symmetrical being . . . it does not happen, but just is"
(p. 101). This depiction of an existential experience of reality,
unelaborated, approximates Winnicott's (1971) notion of
"being," Bion's (1962) notion of "beta elements" (β elements)
or "undigested facts," and Lacan's (1964) notion of the register
of the "real." These are all ways to talk about basic sense data, or
things-in-themselves—what Mitrani (1995) termed "unmentalized

experiences" and Bromberg (1991) described as "unsymbolized experiences." These are primary experiences that have not yet been digested or elaborated in verbal, symbolic terms; untouched as yet by language or its categories. Although these primary experiences are fundamental to any understanding of how meanings develop, they ineluctably elude our attempts at description.

The meanings of these primary experiences are perhaps best approximated through the use of metaphor. Metaphor allows us to look at an essential relationship between elements through the use of an exemplar (Matte-Blanco, 1975). Bion (1963) and Matte-Blanco (1988) each used "metabolic" metaphors when describing transformative processes. Bion (1963), for example, used this type of metaphor in his attempt to describe how primary sensory experience becomes translated into verbal thought. Bion based his theory on the containing and metabolizing functions of the mother, suggesting that this transformation occurs through the ongoing relationships between "container" and "contained," which depend first on the transformation of raw elements through mentation. The undigested (β) element is too concrete and too idiosyncratic to be useful in thinking proper; it must first be transformed into a more generalizable, more abstract element, which will be more tractable.

The presence of patterning suggests that the original sensory data have already been elaborated into "alpha" (α) elements, which "comprise visual images, auditory patterns, olfactory patterns" (Bion, 1962, p. 26), whereby they may be utilized in dreams, unconscious waking thinking, and memory. These patterned elements form the basis of implicit and relational knowings, which may then be brought together to form more complex thoughts. The reversal of this process is the unlinking of associations, which Bion (1962) described as the "beta-screen," roughly corresponding to the position Tustin (1991) described as "pathological autism," versus the more normative position described by Ogden (1989). Alpha function (mentation) enables the individual to utilize experience rather than being faced with the unsatisfactory choice of either taking evasive measures or becoming overwhelmed.

In an attempt to make manifest the relationships between elements without obscuring them by content, Bion (1962) moved to a formalized, abstract system (see also Charles, 2002). Paradoxically, he valorized primary self-experience through the use of symbols that are intentionally chosen because they lack referents in this same experience. In this way, his work highlights the complex interrelationship between the abstract and the concrete that facilitates the elaboration of meaning in their interplay as, alternately, container and contained.

Both abstraction and concretization help to elaborate thought, correlating experience with generalized concepts or further sensory data, respectively. The concrete gives foundational meaning, whereas the abstract helps to make our knowledge more usable. Each becomes a way of recognizing and elucidating patterned elements that come to carry multiple meanings. The capacity to form abstractions enables the individual to move beyond that which is literally known in a derivative sense, to that which *might* be known in the sense of understanding, and facilitates the communication of that knowledge at a verbal level. It can also, however, make it difficult for us to apply this knowledge in concrete, pragmatic ways.

In moving to an abstract algebraic system, Bion (1962) simplified his concepts, but also made them relatively inaccessible. We must then translate the processes he described back into concrete examples in order to integrate them effectively. This translation process ensues in the consulting room, as well. Much of the primary data our patients bring to us is encoded as sensory and affective experience that is patterned in essential ways, but has not been elaborated in asymmetrical categorical terms. At these times it can be the capacity to enact what has eluded verbal understanding that facilitates communication and thereby brings us closer to the understanding we seek (Kumin, 1996).

An example from the consulting room may be useful here, in the form of an attempt to disentangle truth from falsity, progression from obstruction. The distinction between evasion and modification in reaction to pain is a crucial one, but not always easy to make in process. Evasion precludes growth. It "is intended not to affirm but to deny reality, not to represent an emotional experience but to misrepresent it to make it appear to be a fulfillment rather than a striving for fulfillment" (Bion, 1962, p. 49).

If the aim of psychoanalysis is seen as truth, the lying patient may be seen to be in conflict with the analyst. The lie may, however, also be a way of bringing to the attention of the analyst the very defenses within which the patient is caught. In this sense, the lie becomes a potentially useful enactment: a definitory statement of sorts, pointing to the nature of the problem. Recreating essential dilemmas in this way provides patient and analyst with an opportunity to know together what cannot be spoken about, as of yet. It also provides an opportunity to know whether we are moving toward understanding or away from it.

For example, in my work with "David" I wonder, quite actively at times, whether we are in the realm of false statements or lies, and how we might distinguish between the two. This would seem to be an essential dilemma for David: how can he know aspects of himself that he finds so distasteful that they have become virtually unknowable, especially in the face of his determined efforts, over the years, to divorce himself from the self that he would rather not know. On one day, in particular, we found ourselves faced with this dilemma of the lie. He had said, "I don't know," and I asked him whether this was a statement of fact or a statement he was hoping to make fact in the moment or a lie that he was hoping would end the subject. The question seemed important, I said, because it had to do with whether or not he knew what was true, which was much more important than whatever he might or might not tell me. This focus on what David was saying and not saying led to an intensification in the work and an association to a previous lie: in that moment, we were able to join together in our quest for greater understanding (described more fully in Charles, 2002a).

Bion's (1962) formal system helps us to be aware of subtleties within the process—such as the difference between a lie and a lack of awareness—that help us to make sense of what is going on within the process, even when the individual is not able (explicitly) to bring forward the material that troubles him. The material is there: in another form, at another level. It is there metaphorically, an arena with which we have some familiarity. Part of the dance, as we begin to work with a patient, is to discern what might be known and the parameters within which meanings can be established. With David, for example, we have had to agree on basic facts, such as the meanings in the moment of statements such as "I don't know" or "nothing." In this way, we are also having a discussion about the process of analysis and our preconceptions, which do not always agree. From his side, it seems to be a place in which help might be found, but only theoretically (when the reality seems too dire). This hope helps him to persevere in coming to sessions, even though they are often frustrating and ostensibly unproductive.

Bion (1962, 1963) struggled to illuminate these types of essential truths, such as the importance of distinguishing between the lie and falsity. In this quest, he found the relationship between elements to be a crucial factor in understanding. He termed this relationship the "selected fact" and quoted at length from Poincaré's (1952) description of the process of mathematical formulation, by way of illustration:

> If a new result is to have any value, it must unite elements long since known, but till then scattered and seemingly foreign to each other, and suddenly introduce order where the appearance of disorder reigned. Then it enables us to see at a glance each of these elements in the place it occupies in the whole. Not only is the new fact valuable on its own account, but it alone gives value to the old facts it unites. . . . The only facts worthy of our attention are those which introduce order into this complexity and so make it accessible to us [in Bion, 1962, p. 72].

The "selected fact" may be a new term to us, but it is not a new concept. It is our selection of facts—the ways in which we order and give meaning to our experience—that eventuates in our idiosyncratic views of reality. This principle may be seen quite explicitly in the type of figure-ground examples found in the literature on sense perception. It may also be seen, more implicitly, in our interpretations, which highlight our own perceptual biases. Our decisions about how to link, categorize, and value the various bits of information that assail us have profound ramifications for the meanings we attribute. In the consulting room, our interpretations are a way of reframing reality for our patients. They provide new ways of ordering and making salient whatever "selected fact" we are using to ground and organize the material.

The other side of this ordering process is the introduction of disorder—or complexity—into order, which also facilitates the creation of something new. With David, for example, my insistence on creating possible permutations of his statement, rather than merely accepting it, created an initial disorder from which a new order emerged. This interplay may be seen as the dialectic between the paranoid-schizoid and depressive positions, through which real learning can take place. This level of engagement with the material creates the possibility of true comprehension, thereby facilitating further learning.

For Bion (1962), the discovery of a selected fact is always idiosyncratic and affectively driven. He depicted the discovery of coherence (meaning) as a significant event that becomes known through its undeniable impact on the perceiver. Meaning is fundamentally a function of linking, whether of object to object, idea to idea, or self to other (Bion, 1962, 1963). Naming, in whatever form, provides an enduring link between patterned elements, prescribing the order of their interrelationships and thereby facilitating the ongoing task of integration.

TRANSFORMATION AS AN ESSENTIAL ASPECT OF GROWTH AND CREATIVITY

In his explications of the selected fact, Bion (1963) affirmed the importance of fundamental affective knowings that help to organize and give meaning to our experiences. Freud (1915) struggled with these same issues as well, suggesting that sensory data must be linked to words through "traces" in order to be susceptible to conscious thought. However, these meanings exist and can be communicated regardless of whether or not we are able to put them into words. The ability to receive and communicate meanings through divers modalities is an essential underpinning of human growth and creativity, regardless of the extent to which the information is accessible to conscious awareness.

In many creative processes, the sensory data itself becomes form, which is then translated into a medium other than words. Even when the medium is poetry, the transformation is such that the word is not utilized in the same manner as occurs during more traditional thinking and speaking. In psychoanalysis, this process of transformation appears to occur through the type of amodal processing described by Stern (1985) and others (see Edkins, 1997), by which containment enables meaning-making to occur. For example, Winnicott (1977) related how a four-year-old patient told her mother that she didn't need to know what was wrong in order to communicate it to Winnicott, saying: "I don't know, but I can always tell him" (p. 163).

Bion (1965), too, affirmed that transformations in analysis do not occur solely in verbal form. Rather, he suggested that verbal knowing can interfere with the person's ability to actually be in a different place with themselves. Bion (1962) distinguished between knowledge and understanding, positing knowledge as information that imposes order from the outside, whereas understanding is arrived at through one's own experience. Crucial here is whether one's "knowledge" is used in the service of evasion or, alternatively, moves toward growth and greater understanding.

"Knowing about" can become an autistic object, of sorts, a second skin or empty shell that protects one from learning through experience, and thereby from any real knowing or understanding (see chapter 3; see also Balint, 1959). For example, Bion (1963) described a patient whose words did not conform to any coherent rules and therefore functioned as sound rather than as speech. Along with the evasive functions of the sound production, however, there was also, in tandem, a willingness to encounter meaning at the patient's own pace and in his own way. Bion noted that the pattern of sound had meaning for the patient, which could be experienced by him through a form of projective identification, in which the sound was expelled out into the room. Bion's faith that the patient's production had meaning facilitated the patient's ability to enact the meaning he could neither know nor speak to. In this way, meaning was revealed in a form that could be taken in by the patient and then utilized by both patient and analyst in ongoing attempts toward understanding.

DIMENSIONALITY

As in the previous example, there are many primitive experiences that are unconscious, not due to repression, but by virtue of their structure, which cannot become conscious without being transformed in some fashion. Some experiences may not have been integrated in verbal symbolic form, whereas others may not conform or cohere to our habits of thought, being inconsistent with our other thinking, or perhaps too large or small a thought to be grasped. Many theorists have noted that our perspective severely constricts our ability to understand. Matte-Blanco (1975, 1988) described this conceptual limitation in terms of "dimensionality." Restricting our scope enables us to represent complex phenomena by imposing arbitrary orders on them but, in moving to a register of fewer dimensions, we are also misrepresenting them in fundamental ways.

"Reality" is always constrained by our ability to perceive whatever stands before us. Grotstein (2000a) cautioned that "what we call perception is more often apperception . . . the falsification or personalized distortion that underlies the illusion of perception" (p. xxi). Many of our terms, such as "transference," point toward the idiosyncratic nature of perception. Klein's (1957) positions, on the other hand, provide a means for conceptualizing more generalized differences in orientation toward "fact." From the paranoid-schizoid position, the basic form or sensation becomes more richly elaborated, but it is only from the depressive position that the elaboration becomes better integrated and takes on the type of perspective associated with three-dimensional space (Grotstein, 2000b).

As an example, we might look at a patient who continually laments her mother's rejections, until one day she is able to hear my reflections of her own assaultiveness that cause people to recede. Elena had spent years assailing the withholding (uncaring) mother without being able to encounter the human (and essentially caring) one who had reached the limits of her own abilities (Charles, 2001b). In this way, Elena had been caught in the paranoid-schizoid position, unable to integrate good and bad aspects of self or other. Someone had needed to be vile and empty, to stand in opposition to the other, who became the repositor of all that was good and worthy. The sides might shift, but the disjunction remained constant. From the depressive position, in contrast, Elena was able to see her mother's failures (as well as her own) without needing to revile self or other.

There is an ongoing dialectic between these two modes. At one extreme, we have the experience as such; at the other, conscious, rational thought. Many experiences are not accessible to conscious thought, whether because of the age at which they were encoded, the modality in which they were encoded, or the intensity of the associated affect. Although perspective may be an essential precondition for rational understandings, our perspective can also severely constrain these understandings. Many facets of reality may be incomprehensible given our frame of reference, and yet be eminently comprehensible given a wider frame.

Although this seems complex in the abstract, it is something we encounter continually in our daily lives as well as in the consulting room. It is somewhat like those camera shots in which we are first given a magnified view that is difficult to make sense of until the camera pulls back and shows us the context. For example, no process can be understood without the frame of time: omitting that dimension gives lie to the entire concept, making it, literally, incomprehensible. Space has a similar framing function. Many concepts have little meaning isolated from the contexts within which they occur. Procedural knowledge, for example, may only be known within the relevant context.

There would seem to be little about human intrapsychic or interpersonal functioning that is comprehensible without some understanding of context; hence, the requisite associations to dreams or other material in analysis. Without these associations, whatever "meanings" we might deduce are derived more substantively from the context of our own thoughts than from those of the other. Although we might have something useful to add from our own frame of reference, this can only augment, not replace, the individual's own associations.

Matte-Blanco (1988) suggested that dimensionality becomes particularly problematic in regard to unconscious processes, which operate "in a space of a higher number of dimensions than that of our perceptions and conscious thinking" (p. 91). Ironically, we can often understand, through less conscious means, that which becomes incomprehensible or unwieldy when we approach it "logically" or "rationally." In the nonverbal register, we can often find the right key that allows us to pass through time and space to arrive at the relevant destination. Affect, for example, becomes a transducer, permitting intermodal matching of ostensibly unlike experiences.

The concept of multidimensionality affirms the importance of space: of having some perspective from which to observe and to reflect upon one's observations, rather than experiencing them as "fact." This arena has been termed "potential space" by Winnicott (1971), in that it is a prerequisite for any creative endeavor to occur. Winnicott (1971) distinguished poignantly between creative and noncreative thinking in his depiction of the patient who told him: "I have been playing patience for hours in my empty room and the room really is empty because while I am playing patience I do not exist" (p. 36). Crucial to this distinction is the type of dimensionality that allows for some multiplicity of meaning. Winnicott argued that the patient's fantasies were *about* a subject without representing any reflections upon that subject. In contrast, the patient's dream "*had poetry in it,* that is to say, layer upon layer of meaning related to past, present, and future, and to inner and outer, and always fundamentally about herself" (1971, p. 35).

In our analytic work, there is an ongoing struggle to try to bring to conscious awareness these multiple layers of meaning. Bion and Matte-Blanco used different language to refer to this process of moving from unconscious to conscious (from sensory impressions, through ordering, to meaning [knowing rather than knowing-about]) and being able to hold on to each. Bion (1965) referred to this process as a "transformation," whereas Matte-Blanco (1975) depicted it as a "translating" or "unfolding" function. The unconscious can only be brought into consciousness by virtue of its elaboration in spatio-temporal form. The act of creating, within the lived moment, forms that represent, to some extent, our experience of that moment—and thereby contain some essential aspect of it—is one aspect of the transformative process. In this way, we move the experience-as-lived into the spatio-temporal realm through the elaboration of its registration on the senses.

In accord with Bion (1962, 1963), Matte-Blanco (1975) suggested that for the unconscious to become conscious there must be a selection process: we can only know a few finite bits of the infinite at any one time. Words are the asymmetrical tools of the translating/unfolding function, moving from infinite into finite, giving form and structure to that which must be represented in some fashion in order to be communicated. Although we inevitably lose something of the original experience as it becomes contained/constrained, this is an inevitable part of the process of making meaning in the asymmetrical world of verbal interchange.

For Matte-Blanco (1975), the human mind is in a chronic process of extracting form in the interplay of unlike with like. His description of the psychoanalytic process is remarkably similar to Poincaré's (1952) description of the selected fact:

> The action of psycho-analytic therapy consists of divesting persons, things and circumstances from their symbolic

meaning (which leads to the confusion of the individual with the whole class) and transforming them, for conscious thinking, into what they really should be, that is, circumscribed entities in which the halo of the class does not interfere with their concrete meaning, by making them appear more than what they actually are. It is, in short, an action divesting or taking away from the concrete object the infinite set to which it plays host: a process of discharge [Matte-Blanco, 1975, p. 185].

If we see the analytic enterprise as a search for meaning—for understanding—one of our most important tools is our ability to make sense of the multiplicity of cues that present themselves to us in the complex expressions of nonverbal language. Primary experiences often make themselves known through their unique patternings, which come to carry profound yet often elusive meanings. If we attend to the language of the body and allow its patterns to affect us and to thereby inform our understanding, our work is immeasurably enriched. The human facility for amodal perception allows us to integrate essential patterns and to transform them into empathic resonance and verbal language, thereby highlighting and often transforming extant reality.

2

PATTERNS: UNCONSCIOUS SHAPINGS OF SELF AND EXPERIENCE

*I*t is often via enactments that we may discover parts of ourselves, long ago absorbed into the fragments of our beings and stored, often unnoticed, as part of what Bollas (1987) has termed the "unthought known." I have found myself enacting, in many forms, my longings to make sense of whatever cues are provided in a universe always, to some extent, beyond comprehension. The beach has become a forum for this type of enactment, in that my experiences there have the familiar feel of an archaic form emerging toward consciousness. I like to celebrate spring with walks along beaches, basking in the sounds, smells, and sensations of the sea. In these walks, I have become acutely aware of pattern as an organizing principle and perhaps a fundamental truth. On any given beach, my eyes turn toward novelty: toward whatever particular configuration of size, shape, and distribution of color has become "treasure" for that stretch of sand, at that hour, on that day. There have been sojourns of no seashells, in which I have wandered somewhat haphazardly, saddened by the paucity, wondering at the meaning of this withholding by the sea. At times I have dug in the sand, something having caught my eye, and discovered myself in the midst of untold sea treasures in another, deeper layer.

21

Each year I return, never sure how or when the sea will offer up its riches or whether I will discover the key. I marvel at the complexity of pattern, the myriad mutations, distortions, perturbations-yet all seemingly the same at some level of abstraction. As my eyes scan for novelty, skipping over the multitude of unblemished white shells glistening like tiny fingernails, I wonder on what beach these forgotten ones would shine forth, radiant like iridescent jewels. It is rarely the shell itself that commands attention; it is odd to find some unique specimen, awaiting admiration. More often, it is the almost absent-minded scanning, lulled by sun, wind, and surf: the mechanical sifting for unbroken relics of unknown lives.

This attention to pattern bears a metaphoric relation to the analytic endeavor and is also reminiscent of a phrase from a Jewish prayer: "to keep faith with those that sleep in the dust." That phrase always seemed to me to be about patterns as well: to pattern ourselves in some way around those we have loved, that we might carry them with us. Much as a mollusk forms itself around a grain of sand to bring forth a pearl, we form ourselves around our experiences and become shaped by them—at times misshapen, at times ennobled, occasionally bringing forth some pearl—perhaps all of these, at various times, in our own ways. In similar fashion, the face, too, becomes patterned over the years by sorrow and joy, hope and despair, contentment and anger. There is a sifting through of our experience, even in our very visages, that comes to balance somewhere between a porous willingness and an obtruded blindness that can suffer no encroachments.

We seem to make sense of the world through our understandings of sameness and difference, termed "symmetry" and "asymmetry" by Matte-Blanco (1975). From a distance, the beach is largely symmetrical: a field of white sand with little to distinguish it. As we move closer, we begin to notice the asymmetry: to make discriminations within the seeming sameness. There is the larger patterning of the sand itself, which points to where the shells might be hiding, and also the patterning of shells among shells and of each shell within itself. None of these is static, but rather emerges over time in the interplay with wind and water, reflecting and becoming part of the greater order/ disorder.

The analytic endeavor plays out in similar fashion. It is rarely some unique event that holds the key, but rather a new way of seeing repetitive themes that had eluded our understanding. We often begin at a point of ostensible sameness and then discover aspects of the other that distinguish him or her as an individual with a unique narrative, perceptions, and experiences. Alternatively, we might begin at a point of seeming disjunction, whereby the person before us appears as "other," and the work entails the discovery of points of commonality amidst the differences. Each vantage is essential for knowing both self and other.

In this chapter, I will consider ways in which pattern becomes a means for facilitating growth and understanding. From the early rhythms of experience[1] that configure the world for the infant, to the prosodies of affect and the tectonics of unconscious fantasy that give meaning and richness to our experience, pattern would seem to be our basic way of understanding self, other, and world. There is comfort in the pattern: it becomes the known. However, there also tends to be a lack of plasticity in, and a lack of awareness of, that which is known at that level.

Growth would seem to necessitate a continual dialectic between like and unlike, known and unknown, inside and outside. Internal patternings of the body become templates for external reality, much as Erikson (1950) depicted, while external patternings of darkness and light, pain and comfort, become templates for our internal reality. Basic patterns become units of meaning, which may be transposed from one modality to another and yet be inherently recognizable in terms of their fundamental meanings. These patterns may be highly elusive to our normal, rational sense of what might be termed "meaningful."

---

1. The interested reader is referred to Ryavec (1998) for further elaborations of this theme.

They are most often registered, and thereby may best become known, affectively, forming the basis of unconscious fantasies that structure our experiences of the world (Isaacs, 1948). As we attempt to grapple with these patternings, the language, metaphors, and algorithms of recent scientific and mathematical elucidations provide a rubric through which we might enhance our understanding, as well as our ability to communicate these elusive realities to our patients.

MODELS FOR UNDERSTANDING ELUSIVE REALITIES

In psychoanalysis, as in physics, much of what we study is literally incomprehensible. Just as quantum theory attempts to make sense of patterns inherent in forces we cannot discern through the senses, so, too, does psychoanalytic theory attempt to throw light on aspects of experience that are outside the reaches of conscious reflection. According to quantum theory, the subatomic discontinuous events themselves are unvisualizable. We must "invent" or "idea-lize" them in order to be able to think about them or communicate our ideas about them (Bohr, 1934). They are, in this sense, created by us: we never see the essential building blocks, which are beyond our perception. The basic processes themselves are literally inconceivable "to a mind whose physical concepts are derived from the familiar properties of its quotidian forms of perception—especially position, momentum, energy, and time" (Opatow, 1997, p. 291).

What we do see is the order/disorder created by them: the pattern. Inspiration often comes in the form of pattern. Creativity entails an application of the "intuition" to a seemingly unrelated problem. Although intuition is often discredited, it is a quintessential human function, in which we come to understand aspects of experience that are relatively inaccessible by rational, logical mind. Einstein is quoted as saying "I very rarely think in words at all. A thought comes and I may try to express it in words afterwards . . . . All our thinking is in the nature of a free play of concepts" (in Opatow, 1997, p. 292).

Our models say much about our values: many attempts to

integrate psychoanalytic thinking with information gained through advances in science and mathematics have been rejected as "unscientific." It is true that we often mistake a scientific or mathematical formulation for "truth" (Denman, 1994) and yet

> the strategy of noting the pervasiveness of a certain basic . . . form in nature, and inferring that it supports the explanatory claims of whatever hypotheses show particular phenomena to exhibit that form, is a general strategy of reasoning in science that is widely employed and uncontentiously reputable [Gardner, 1994, p. 223].

Although these formulations are largely unprovable, they may be singularly evocative in terms of their impact on how we think about psychoanalysis. This type of resistance to potentially useful new rubrics has plagued the history of knowledge. However,

> if the different branches of knowledge can be viewed as explicate order phenomena unfolded from the total holomovement of human thought, it becomes possible to use connexions which have been rejected in the past as irrational or unscientific. In particular, meaning is just as valid as scientific proof, and thought needs to be anchored in one person's experience [Arden, 1985, p. 479].

In some measure, our attempts to move beyond the ostensibly personal (the subjective) may be seen as homage unproductively paid to our notions of "science," which are, indeed, as subjective as any other system we might posit. It is, paradoxically, at once a denial of our own subjectivity and its value, and an act of extraordinary hubris.

Discoveries in quantum physics affirm the inherent, and consensually unconfirmable, uniqueness of the individual perspective (Bohr, 1958). Individual experience is often likened to that of chaotic systems, both of which rely on initial conditions (Kincanon and Powel, 1995) and are therefore at once determined and unpredictable, making it difficult to arrive at other than generalized rules (Priel and Schreiber, 1994). To truly understand the determinants of the individual's experience, we must turn, as Arden (1985) suggested, to the individual. Although our theories give us ideas about where to look, they do not take the place of attention to idiosyncratic patternings. To the contrary, assumptions regarding the nature of "order" often impede our ability to discern it. For example, in chaotic systems, "the emergence of order is often accompanied by the appearance of spatially asymmetric patterns" (Nicolis and Prigogine, 1981, p. 659), which seem to be particularly difficult for us to comprehend.

Pattern inheres in nature. It is present, whether or not we can discern or make use of it. Bohm (1980) referred to a relational or "implicate" order, holographic[2] in form, which contains within each piece the form of the whole. The essential pattern is not reducible to component parts, but exists as a gestalt, rather like a musical theme that can be played and replayed with variations in tempo, phrasing, instrument, and key and yet may be recognizable in form.

Notably, form is always a function of the observer; physicists have shown that the observation of a process changes it and that consciousness itself affects the process (Bohr, 1958). We can never *see* the unobserved data. For all intents and purposes, it does not exist as such, but only insofar as it has registered upon the senses (or some intermediary instrument) from which we make deductions about the past and predictions about the future (Bohm, 1965).

Our formulations are based on the patterns abstracted from our experience. Matte-Blanco (1975) depicted consciousness rather like the computer, in that it reduces reality to the patternings of two elements: yes or not-yes, same or not-same.

---

2. Notably, "holograph" refers both to a three-dimensional image and to a text written wholly by hand: an individual narrative. Although I refer to the visual field, Bohm refers more generally to "holomovement": the multidimensional patterning or rhythmicity underlying order and meaning.

Unlike the computer, however, this reality has consciousness overarching it, intruding into it, organizing it (Penrose, 1994). The life sciences can never be understood solely in terms of disparate parts, but rather in terms of the relations among those parts. Increasing differentiation is an inherent aspect of the living being; growth "is not merely revelatory, it is the generation of form" (Ingold, 1990, p. 215).

Brennan (1997) compared the inherent dialectic between life and death—between growth and degeneration—to the dichotomy between sameness and difference, wherein death results, ultimately, in sameness: a complete lack of differentiation: the "homogenization of form" (p. 259). As energy becomes bound, it is less accessible: the organism becomes less flexible, less resilient, less amenable to change (Brennan, 1997). So, too, as the image or idea becomes bound—or "saturated," as Bion (1970) put it—it becomes fixed and rigid, and difficult to think about. Brennan (1997) suggested that these fixities lead to degeneration: to death. They certainly appear to lead to the death of mind as an active process: the more fixed the idea, the less room there is for reflection.

We are imperfect instruments, at best. In psychoanalysis, as in physics,

> it is the conscious application of these categories of experience and reason that brings the world to order. But these concepts are imposed by the nature of our mental apparatus and are not features of the world-in-itself, the world without us. . . . for psychoanalysis, there is also a mental world which underlies the world of (introspective) appearances and is, as it were, an inner world without us [Opatow, 1997, p. 296].

Our unconscious fantasies become patterns, or algorithms, that structure our experiences (Isaacs, 1948) in ways that conscious mind then seeks to comprehend (Penrose, 1989).

Opatow (1997) suggested that the "new" physics affirms a basic proposition of Spinoza (1677) that "the order and connection of ideas is the same as the order and connection of things" (Book 2, Prop. 7). From this it would follow that whatever causes exist, do so apart from our ability to discern those causes and yet may become more accessible to us through our theories. In psychoanalysis, our basic data—the other's sensory experience—is itself always beyond our grasp. We are left to intuit it from whatever data may be communicated to us by the patient. This becomes a palimpsest—or overlay—on our theory, which in turn overlays our own experiences as we have come to know them. At a fundamental level, what becomes communicated is pattern, translated by each individual via his or her own unique idioms.

PATTERNS AS BUILDING BLOCKS OF EXPERIENCE

Pattern would seem to be a primary unit of meaning. From the earliest moments of life, we are impinged upon by patterns that become organized over time into complex narratives of self, other, and world. Arden (1985) noted the primacy of pattern in human experience: "rational thinking about space, time, and causality have to be learned by the infant, whereas the awareness of movement is present from the beginning" (p. 475). Our earliest experiences are of the body, interpreted through the "nameless entities which are constellations of sensation" (Tustin, 1969, p. 32) that become known, organized, and named over time. The patternings of rhythmicity and constancy, in their essence, become the units of meaning that inform all later understanding.

As symbolic functions develop, they tend to push the more primary, sensory aspects of knowing to the background. These nonverbal understandings become, to some extent, disowned and thereby less comprehensible. However, the patterns of experience, built up through impingements on the perceptual systems, are "remembered," even though they may be too complex to be comprehended fully in the moment. The constraints of dimensionality come into play here. Our sensoria are inadequate to the task of understanding our own complexity. We can look at one small system in fine-grained detail (and delude ourselves

with the illusion of the "completeness" of our understanding),
but as we move farther away—in an attempt to understand the
interrelationships among the parts—we lose the detail and are
left with our amazement at the utter complexity of the system.

Our less conscious mind appears to grapple better with the
confluence of detail with complexity. In our dreams or in so-
called "oceanic experiences," we have a sense of the imminent
order in the totality, the patterns governing the motions and
interrelations of the parts. This, however, is not easily translat-
able into language, secondary process phenomena. What we
are left with is a sense of patterned order, which underlies our
faith that if we attend carefully enough, we can translate the
patterns we have observed and encoded, in whatever modality,
into their verbal counterpart, from whence we might "make
sense" of them and manipulate them toward that end we term
"understanding."

Affect is one means of "knowing" pattern. It has long been
noted for its signal functions (Freud, 1926), which provide cues
for danger, yet also perpetuate the illusion of danger when it
has passed. Affect, fundamentally, is about patterns of light and
dark, crescendo and decrescendo: expectations, meetings, and
disappointments. We carry these patterns within us beyond what
may be "known" about them in any given instance. Affect provides an experiential sense of knowing, from whence "knowing
about" may become elaborated through the interchange of
words between analyst and analysand regarding their disparate
interpretations of shared experiences.

Through countertransference experiences of being with the
other in the moment, the analyst may come to know the patterns
of the other. These patterns may be manifested in highly indi-
vidualized and personalized ways—much like pieces of dreams—
and yet, over time, they take the form of recognizable symbols
that we know through their affective configurations. These configurations, in turn, become recognizable as equivalent for that
individual via other imagery, metaphors, and experiences that
have the same configural quality, in that they are composed of
similar patterns in different keys, tones, or modalities.

To the extent that our knowing is nonverbal, it may be difficult to hold meanings in mind, much less communicate them. The associative process offers an opportunity for the relatively free play of pattern upon pattern, whereby meaning becomes further elaborated through the metaphors that have become imbued with meanings configured by the history of ongoing interactions between patient and analyst. As affect becomes intensified, however, distinguishing gradations tend to disappear and the class of equivalents (or "sets") moves toward infinity (Matte-Blanco, 1975). At that point, the experience of knowing precludes knowing-about. There is no perspective from which to consider either similarities or differences.

It is through secondary process, or "asymmetrical logic" (Matte-Blanco, 1975), that we make sense of our experience by establishing distinctions between like things. This ability is essential for the elaboration of consensual symbols. Segal (1957) described symbol formation as a process of organizing emergent asymmetries within the object world. The first symbols are experienced as objects—"symbolic equations"—with no distinctions made between symbol and object (Klein, 1930). As development progresses, however, distinctions emerge and the symbol comes to *represent* the object, rather than being equated with it. Symbol formation serves to integrate internal and external realities, providing the dimensionality required for verbal thinking and communication (Segal, 1957). The drive toward making meaning is a fundamental aspect of being human, welling from an "internal necessity for inner organization, pattern, coherence, the basic need to discover identity in difference without which experience becomes chaos" (Milner, 1952, p. 84).

Meaning is derived contextually, within the rubric of relationships. Pulls toward being like or unlike the other become unconscious patterns guiding our perceptions. This patterning is a reciprocal process, whereby the self becomes patterned by and onto experience. As Bollas (1992) described it:

Each of us at birth is equipped with a unique idiom of psychic organization that constitutes the core of our self, and then in the subsequent first years of our life we become our parents' child, instructed by the implicate logic of their unconscious relational intelligence in the family's way of being: we become a complex theory for being a self that the toddler does not think about but acquires operationally [p. 51].

The parent's reality is interposed over and into the experience of the child, becoming her reality, as well. In this way, repetitive themes become patterned upon the lives of successive generations (Shabad, 1993). The constrictions limiting the affective experience of the parent become restrictions on the child, who ingests them in turn as fundamentally her own, even when she rejects them in principle, thereby confounding reality to an extraordinary degree. This was the case with "Sophia," to follow. Beneath the ostensible rejection of the bad mother, she fits like another skin and we walk inside of her, albeit unknowing, save for our less conscious recesses, which note the patterns and fear discovery when we encounter a like form. It is often the mother in ourselves of whom we fear discovery: in the patterning of affective colorations we know this intuitively, at a less than conscious level. As Shabad (1993) has described, the dissimilarity of content often masks the similarity of structure in these types of reenactments.

As analysts, we tend to configure ourselves according to the patterns of our patients' modes of being in the world. What has been termed "empathy" may be seen as a complex attempt to configure ourselves affectively to the inner workings of an other's being. In this way, we learn to resonate with the particular nuances of that individual's experience of their inner and outer worlds. We are imperfect instruments at best, and yet our attempts to tune ourselves in their key provides a bridge that facilitates the transmission of meaning from one person to another. This ability to tune one's self to the other has its origins within the family, in the early interactions between caretaker and child that become prototypical "dance steps" guiding subsequent interactions (Freud, 1921; Bion, 1961; Charles, 1999a).

Individuals tend to take on roles in accordance with the con-figurations defined in their families of origin. The family con-stellation, itself, becomes a pattern that prescribes and proscribes future development (Charles, 1999a). As Bollas (1992) has sug-gested, the self becomes known in the interplay of the parents' reality onto the experience of the child. In this way, repetitive themes of both family and culture become patterned upon the lives of successive generations (Shabad, 1993; Charles, 2000a). At some level, we are always trying to identify or disidentify with a parent or sibling representation. The assumption of these roles entails a disowning of aspects of self that have been defined as "not-me" within that relationship (Charles, 2001c). As facets of self become not-known, they can be neither fully utilized nor developed. We become crippled by our blindness to facets of self that are beyond our purview and are often integrated at a very primitive level, thereby compounding their relative inac-cessibility (Bion, 1967).

CASE ILLUSTRATIONS

Patterned experiences often propel our movements in complex ways that may be difficult to discern. The analyst's ability to observe and communicate patterns may offer crucial insights that facilitate growth. For example, Sophia struggled against the pattern she had learned to identify as "mother." This pattern had taken the form of powerful and hostile critical others whose reality must prevail in any given moment. My patient learned to survive by her vigilance for this particular configuration in her environment, toward which she assumed the complementary pattern, which she termed "lying low." Hiding in this way ensured her survival. However, it also violated her own boundaries and sense of self. At a fundamental level, she was "re-configured" in the presence of dangerous others. Sophia's experience in the wake of these meetings had been one of relief at survival, as well as a sense of having lost her self, which she described as feeling "dissociated" or "distant" from herself. This was experienced as both a loss and a failure: she longed to be able to maintain her-self in the presence of these powerful others.

Over the course of our work together, I tracked within *my* sensoria ebbs and flows in Sophia's presence/absence. Communicating these impressions to Sophia helped her to become more aware of how profoundly she would lose herself. As her determination to remain present grew, she worked diligently toward better understanding impediments to her own self-acceptance. In an encounter with an extremely hostile and annihilating mother figure, Sophia was able, in spite of almost incapacitating fear, to meet the feared "mother" in the presence of a supportive "mother." This confirmed her own reality, thereby better enabling her to face her fears regarding her ability to withstand threatened annihilation (described more fully in Charles, 1999a). That experience, by changing the expected pattern, left her feeling more fully herself than had hitherto been her experience. What had been unknowable was how much of herself had been configured in her mother's image. It had been crucial to Sophia to see herself as wholly unlike her mother. My ability to accept *both* the symmetry and the asymmetry helped Sophia to acknowledge the powerful "mother" parts of her own self that at times frighten and intimidate others, while also being aware of the disjunction. For Sophia, these similarities were tempered by the greater empathy and self- and other awareness that make her unlike her mother.

Even Sophia's experience of herself as a physical being had been patterned by her mother's views. In the early days of our work together, Sophia found it difficult to experience her own corporeality. Her mother had seen her as "too big" and had therefore restricted her eating, making bodily needs both vitally important to fill and also so shameful that they were in many ways below conscious awareness. My awareness of her corporeal and sensory absence became an invitation to Sophia to begin to be more interested in attending to her own bodily cues, needs, and experience, rather than viewing them as something alien, to suppress or control. As she became better able to acknowledge and speak to her shame and concomitant dissociation from her body, what had previously been a regimented control over eating and an enforced acceptance of her own shape and size moved toward a greater comfort and fluidity with both the inner and outer experiences of her corporeal self. As she faced her fears of annihilation, patterned after those of her parents, Sophia found herself to be moored, not so uncomfortably nor dangerously, in her own body; in her own reality.

I worked with another woman, "Grace," whose mother could not tolerate the existence of another female in the house. Grace appears to have been designated inherently "bad" and "incapable," a position from which she struggled hopelessly. She both longed for and feared the annihilation of her self, as she lay hidden in her "womb/tomb," seeking oblivion/salvation. The prescribed pills she abused became a means toward losing self while moving within the world, so that she might not know herself and yet might function in some fashion. It was as though she needed to create of herself a not-self—much like a robot—in order to be able to function at all. Not-knowing became a denial of both self and meaning, whereas being able to reflect upon the self became an annihilation of the safety of not-thinking.

Grace tended to shut off *my* thinking, as well, vilifying herself with her own self-loathing commentary, projected into me. I often felt shut out, and one day wondered aloud whether that was in counterpoint to her own feelings of being locked away in her self-imposed prison. Grace was surprised by this interpretation and said reflectively, "I never thought of myself as locked away." In that image lay the seed of a new conception of self: the old pattern could not contain this new image, but had to be broken and reformed to contain this new piece of reality.

In this way, a new image intrudes into the patterns of thinking about the self, causing a ripple in the image—in Bion's (1967, 1970) terms, an "unlinking" or desaturation[3]—through which new conceptions become possible. This type of unlinking opens up the transitional space, in which new configurations may be imagined and tested against what is known or might be

---

3. Bion uses the term saturation to indicate a state in which the presumption of meaning is so absolute and unyielding that there is no room for reflection or amplification. In this way, it becomes closed and static, a presumption that precludes understanding rather than aiding it.

known (Winnicott, 1971). That which had been known is no longer known in quite the same way, in that it is open to inter-pretation and re-interpretation (see Symington, 1983). The pat-tern of the life narrative is no longer fixed and immutable, but rather is open to being reworked, allowing new awareness; new understanding.

As aspects of self become entrenched, they *become* self, as though they were innate characteristics: the ground or given, which may be struggled with or moderated, but always as if with something inherently fixed and unchangeable. The resulting dichotomies are such that any middle ground becomes essen-tially unseen, much as has been described by Ryavec (1997) regarding the process of splitting. As the self becomes divided into the provinces of "me" and "not-me," that which is defined as not-me is not-seen within the bounds of the self, but only out-side. Paradoxically, this rejection also becomes an opportunity for growth. At a deeply unconscious level we play out the pat-terns that have become literally incomprehensible to us, in our attempts to master the trauma associated with them. Matte-Blanco's (1975, 1988) framework of bi-logic offers one structure within which to understand rules inherent in these patterns, and to thereby speak to them with our patients, facilitating their abil-ity to "know what they do."

By way of a more extensive example, I will draw from my work with "Simon," who was faced, at the age of 15 months, with the incomprehensible loss of his mother, through suicide. Simon's last experience of his mother was of being placed in his grand-mother's arms. The rest was absence, which extended out into time and had no end. That pattern had been a profound "back-ground presence" (Grotstein, 1980), moving and shaping our work together. This young man was raised by a series of "moth-ers," all of whom became lost to him in one way or another: from his grandmother who needed him to need her, to two step-mothers who were not able to persist within his object world.

This loss was so intense that the loss of the other became equivalent to the loss of self. In this way, all important relation-ships became invested with potentially devastating significance.

There was fierce rivalry and a concomitant diminishment of self in the face of one stepbrother, in particular, who was seen as victor in the war over both mother and father. Simon and I had been working, at the time being reported, four times weekly for three and a half years. Simon and I sat face to face. He seemed to need that reassurance, because the fear of "losing" me was an ongoing difficulty for him. He anxiously sought the reassurance of my gaze at the beginning of each session and was exquisitely sensitive to shifts in my attention. The space becomes empty very easily in the absence of the mother's gaze.

The metaphor of "patterns" had been an ongoing and important theme in our work together. Simon felt very heavily the weight of his family history, as though condemned by it. He became lost within what he termed his "depression" as though were a cloak, which, once given, would inevitably adhere to his being, like an unwanted second skin. He had found it very difficult to find *himself* within the very real constraints and deprivations of his history.

As Simon neared graduation from university, we were faced quite inexorably with the issue of loss, which he tried desperately to avoid. The sense that parting was imminent was palpable affectively before it began to be apparent in his words. Simon was "moving away" affectively as well as literally, evoking in him tremendous yearnings for closeness. I tried to speak with him about my sense of the imminence of his leaving, but he could not even assimilate my words. It took a great deal of talking between us for them to take hold in his mind and to become thoughts on which he could reflect.

I suggested that he had hoped to not have to face the pain of leaving, and yet there was important work to be done in facing that loss together, in a way that had never been possible for him with previous losses, particularly that of his mother. This is a young man who had been faced with a succession of losses with no acknowledgment and no opportunity to grieve. His vulnerability became the stigmata marking him as lesser than his stepbrother and as a failure in his father's eyes. At that point in the work, Simon appeared to feel caught between the external demands of father/stepbrother and mother/analyst, and so I told him that I didn't need him to stay, but rather that it was important for him to be able to choose what he wanted: to truly choose.

His prospective journey to study abroad represented a crucible for Simon, in which he might finally prove his manhood to his father/self. He felt called upon to accept this challenge, which I likened to a duel, suggesting that he could decide whether or not he wanted to take on that fight: whether it was to be *his* fight. Simon spent a great deal of time in rather tortured silence and by the end of the hour was disgruntled. I had put before him this ultimatum, he said, by giving him a choice: by *making* it a choice. What was hard, he said, was that in being in the presence of someone he trusted, to whom he clearly mattered, he was forced to face the possibility of mattering at all.[4]

"Now," he said, with some chagrin, "I'm going to *have* to celebrate my 'birth' day, and tell people I'm leaving, and not just slip away." He had wanted to split off the pain of prospective losses, much as he had had to split off the pain of the losses of the succession of mothers who had come into his life over the years and of the loss of self inherent in the impossibility of being valued in his home(s) of origin.

Simon began the following session by again referring to his fascination with mattering to me, and the possibility of finding that mattering for *himself*, through me. I suggested that it was important for him to be able to just disappear, which seemed to carry the face of his mother. In this way, he both avoided being left and also tried to find her. He didn't understand and so I said that there were times when we identify with people as a way of making sense of them, kind of like we play "dress-up" as children, as a way of knowing/being our parents, and that we do it in other ways, as well.

"It was a way for you to keep her with you," I said. He was silent for a long time, and the air was very heavy. The enormity

---

4. The interested reader is referred to Parsons (1988) for his treatment of the theme of "mattering."

of his mother's abandonment was too huge and he had so wanted it to not matter: to not annihilate him. I said that it is terrifying to all of us to lose our mothers, yet most of us are able to refind enough of her to enable us to go on.

"So I keep looking for her?" he asked.

"She wasn't there to be refound," I replied, "and becoming her has been a way of not feeling the pain of that."

Simon sat in silence for some time. As we came near the end of the session, I wondered how he was doing. I was concerned that I might have put before him more than he would be able to tolerate. He surprised me, once again, by his extraordinary faith and willingness to try.

"How do you feel?" I asked.

"I feel alive," he said. "Like I can see. Like I could maybe understand this thing. I'm afraid of getting lost in this feeling that no one's going to be there. It's too deep—it's too frightening—it feels way too real."

We encountered this same pattern in Simon's romantic involvements, as well: he tended to lose *himself* in his attempts to find the other. It was as though if he could just be the right way, say the right things, form himself into the normal or acceptable pattern, then, finally, he could be loved. In this way, he would be safe, but he would be lost, as well, which became, for him, the impossible dilemma.

Simon spoke of patterning himself according to the fantasied needs and wishes of a girl with whom he was trying to build a relationship. He would speak into her relative silence, wondering what to make of it. I sensed he was also speaking of my silence, wanting to form himself in my image. My reluctance to give him the coordinates within which to locate himself in space and time frustrated him and made him feel abandoned. When he said he wanted to understand the relationship through her eyes and wished she would just tell him what she wants, I asked him what *he* wanted. Simon responded that he would like to know where she is, but was too frightened of the silence that might ensue if he were to speak. He also feared she would be critical. When I asked whose voice he fears, his thoughts turned to his second step-mother, who would often yell at him for wanting something she could not give. Simon has tried to become that which might be valued, as though he could not be valued for himself. The possibility of being valued as he is had been unimaginable, but was now becoming a glimmer at the periphery of his consciousness: beckoning, just out of reach.

Simon recounted to me a scene from a movie he had watched repeatedly: "There is this one scene," he said, "in *Red*, where the young woman is talking to the old man. She wants to leave, to cross the channel, but is afraid to leave her brother. 'You must just *be*,' the old man tells her."

She is puzzled and doesn't understand, just as my patient was puzzled and did not understand. I suggested that he seemed to be needing to hear what the old man is saying many times because it is so hard for him to imagine that he could, indeed, *be*, nor how that might happen. Simon sat musing in his chair. Unlike previous times, when the silence had felt intolerable to him, this silence had great life and vitality to it.

After some time had passed, he said, "I'm finally understanding thinking as an active thing." Simon was sitting in the silence, being. It was an alive, profound, and vital process and he was not alone in it. He then said that at times he wanted his girlfriend to disappear so he could start again without the pain of loss.

"Kind of like you wanted to slip away so that I would disappear?" I asked. He grinned, a bit sheepishly, his eyes alight.

"Yeah," he said, "I guess I did."

"It's hard to imagine you could leave without the loss being too terrible to endure."

"I think I'm afraid that *I'll* disappear."

"It must have felt that way to you when your mother disappeared," I said, as we sat, resonating quite profoundly with the enormity of his mother's abandonment.

Subsequently, Simon began to talk about ways in which he found himself configuring to the pattern of his father, as well: in particular, to his father's "worrying." Simon had become aware of his own worrying and was uncertain as to how much of this was his own and how much configures to his father. I suggested that this worrying is a way of aligning with his father, of being with him/being him.

As his father worried about Simon's future, Simon struggled with his own fears. He told me about a graduate student friend who had found her own way and was content with the path she had taken: it seemed to be *hers*. In similar fashion, Simon was trying to have faith that his own inner voice would guide him in a direction that would ultimately be right for him, even if the path seemed uncertain. In the midst of his uncertainty came the fears of his father, flying at him from many directions, encircling his own inner voice and leaving the threads very unclear. Simon had decided to leave for the Middle East to study Arabic for the summer, even though he was more interested in studying history than the language—the domain of his father, a language teacher.

This intensive journey into the language itself appeared to be the crucible within which Simon would set himself against his father's measure, in an attempt to finally pass the test he had failed so long ago, standing in the park, being beaten by his stepbrother under his father's distant, disapproving stare. We had come to a greater appreciation of the threads of the father's approbation, which encircle and trip him over and over again. His father's fear that his son would not succeed—that he would not be able to find a place in the world—had become a palpable reality that Simon hoped to reconfigure.

As we talked about his imminent departure, Simon struggled between his own goals and those of his father, exemplified in his desire to finish our work—which had become an affirmation of the value of his own being—versus the need to get a job to affirm his value in his father's eyes. He talked about his intention to return to our work in the fall, after his Middle East journey and a subsequent interlude in the mountains of his father's home, and his hopes to stand on equal ground and to finally put to rest this demand to stand silent in the face of his father.

That summer seemed to be Simon's quest for the holy grail, for the meaning behind the faith of his fathers (and mothers). He sought to understand it in its own language, so that he might be able to find his own meaning from it, rather than having to ingest it predigested, already transformed. Simon was searching to re-pattern his experience: to understand it in new ways. Bollas (1992) has spoken evocatively of this patterning of the self as a kind of psychic journey, in which we configure ourselves to the forms already inherent in our universe, to discover our selves from within them:

> To my mind, the choice of form is a kind of psychic route, as each subject, possessing many different forms for the collecting of experience, renders himself in a different medium, so that playing with the forms means simultaneously being played by them. The choice of representational form is an important unconscious decision about the structuring of lived experience, and is part of the differential erotics of everyday life [p. 41].

Simon's dilemma came to the forefront in a session that was largely about faith: about how we move beyond the illusion of the "reality" of it, to the enormity of choosing it. Simon talked about how he had lost the faith of childhood, which had prescribed and proscribed his existence, thereby evoking for him the illusion of ultimate safety. He found himself searching more strongly for himself—for the self within the self he/they have created—trying to believe that this self could withstand whatever slings and arrows might be incurred. He said he wished that he felt better; when he feels better he can be more daring and speak more largely from his own perspective. I suggested that he was more willing to *be* those parts of himself, whereas there are other parts he would rather disown. At that point, his eyes engaged mine and a faint smile of irony played across his face, as though he knew he was stuck with those pieces he wished not to have.

I found myself thinking of the legend of Merlin, which had figured in our discussions previously. In that legend, the magic had been fed on faith and disappeared without it. Simon had begun the session talking about faith and was now ending it on the same note, but the faith he needed was in himself. I said that, paradoxically, he was creating exactly what he didn't want. He wanted to be his own frame of reference and yet was unwilling to be where he was and how he was, in the face of his fantasies of being judged by me. In his unwillingness to *be*, he was annihilating himself, creating a god of judgment who killed off pieces of him that had been deemed unacceptable. Simon seemed to be trapped by his own vilification of self, which had been introjected from others and then projected back on them, until the bonds were so tightly knit that they became one virtually unseeable "reality." I imagine we are all caught in this web: yearning to be seen, but only partially, as though there were pieces that would annihilate whatever is deemed worthy: whatever might be loved or valued.

CONCLUSION

Bion's (1967) discussions of the interrelationships between the container and the contained provide a rubric within which to better understand the tension between how we become contained and patterned by our experiences and how we, in turn, transform those very containers. Within this model, fragmentation of the old reality provides a framework from which a new reality might emerge. Simon's early experiences provided him with little sense of being held within the object world, which left him highly susceptible to becoming overwhelmed by experiences of loss and emptiness (Grotstein, 1991; Charles, 2000b,c). However, as we came to appreciate and acknowledge the profoundness and the complex ramifications of the losses this young man had experienced, his sense of his own inherent possibilities—affirmed and contained within the analytic hour, within the analyst's mind—became more and more palpable to him as time went by. There emerged the image of a mother/lover who does not leave, standing beside the wraith of the mother/lover who disappears, over and over, interminably. Entwined with this image was one of a self that does not leave, but ebbs, flows, and transforms, containing the old, but also containing the seeds of the new, evolving and becoming more palpably present as he envisions and thereby "real-izes" them.

My work with Simon was informed by Bion's (1967) notions of containing the inconceivable and also by Matte-Blanco's (1975, 1988) depictions of a structure within which the inconceivable might be conceptualized. These conceptualizations provided a framework within which to better elucidate to my patient the patterns that defined and proscribed his experience. The unconscious patterning had been so strong in this young man and so willfully denied that he had little way of seeing the forces that moved him so vitally. My understanding of what Matte-Blanco (1975, 1988) termed the realms of symmetry and asymmetry helped me to put before Simon patterns of his existence in a fashion that brought them into striking relief for him, whereby he, too, could see and struggle with them without being crushed by them. In the past, the repetitive nature of his experience had felt like a weight that could not be borne, as though his history had condemned him to a life of perpetual misery. In successive iterations, however, the pattern had become both more palpable and also lighter. The terrible density had been relieved and he could see through the patterning to new possibilities. Being able to see the intensity of the affect as a chain to the pattern helped Simon to separate the two enough to be able to envision alternatives. Being able to think more fully about his experience helped him to discriminate the asymmetry of past and present, thereby enabling him to envision a future without becoming lost in the condensation of present into past.

Within the analytic hour, the ability to experience both the similarities within differences and the differences within similarities is crucial for the development of an autonomous self capable of real and meaningful engagement with others. This capacity for understanding the regularities within one's own emotional functioning is only possible in an environment in which both anxiety and ambiguity can be contained. From these ensue, as detailed by Winnicott (1971), the capacity to survive.

This capacity is built, among other things, from establishing a rhythm that after dying comes living and vice
versa, after presence comes absence and vice versa
(Ryavec [1998]). It involves both primitive process and
asymmetrical thinking because primitive process contains
the experience of hope and asymmetrical thinking the
concept of a future [Ryavec, 1997, p. 620].

Matte-Blanco's (1975, 1988) elaborations of Freud's (1900,
1915) original conceptions of the unconscious help to elucidate
ways in which the properties of unconscious logic manifest themselves in our daily lives, particularly in those realms more highly
saturated with emotion, in which the laws of the unconscious
hold sway in clear, direct, and palpable form. From Matte-
Blanco's (1975, 1988) perspective, the unconscious adheres to
its own logic, which is quite distinct from the more conventional,
"asymmetrical," logic that dominates conscious thought.
Asymmetry is the domain of distinctions: in asymmetrical logic,
there are specified relationships that are not necessarily
reversible. For example, A is the father of B does *not* mean that
B is the father of A.

In contrast, "symmetrical" logic dominates the unconscious,
wherein the conditions noted by Freud (1915), such as displacement, condensation, timelessness, the absence of mutual
contradiction and negation, and the replacement of external by
internal reality, "sometimes designated as literal interpretation
of metaphor" (Matte-Blanco, 1959, p. 2), rule. Symmetry is the
domain of similarity among seemingly unlike things, in which
the part becomes the whole: in this realm, as Simon patterns
himself on his father, he *becomes* the father.

Noting the logic of the unconscious facilitates our ability to
understand rules and regularities that inhere, much as was made
possible by virtue of Freud's explication of these regularities in
the realm of dreams. All thought contains some admixture of
symmetrical and asymmetrical thought. As affect intensifies, however, symmetrical thought tends to predominate, resulting in a
relative incapacity to distinguish differences between similar

objects (Matte-Blanco, 1975). This condensation of meaning results in overinclusive classes, in which important distinctions cannot be made. One example of symmetrization would be transference, when the analyst, in the moment, becomes the mother, and the patient has difficulty distinguishing between the two. Even though, at some level, they are clearly not the same person, they may be experienced as such: as Simon contemplates leaving me and our work, I become the mother who abandons him endlessly. The task then becomes to focus on the asymmetry —the differences within the sameness—so that we can think about and come to understand the intrusion, rather than merely being overwhelmed and overcome by it.

In this way, any event that is highly saturated in affect tends to work against asymmetrical, or conventionally logical, thought. "Extreme emotional states display qualities of irradiation, maximalization and time and space tend to disappear. . . . at its height grief irradiates, everything good is felt as lost for all eternity" (Rayner, 1981, p. 409). Conversely, the denial of affect precludes any real engagement with others. Both symmetry and asymmetry are necessary for empathic understanding in which neither self nor other is lost. The analytic task entails becoming able to think about an experience while also feeling it.

Grotstein (personal communication, May, 1998) suggested, in the terms of chaos theory, that the unconscious works "according to the laws of the *irrational*," which modern science and mathematics have shown, do, indeed, have their own extraordinary —and yet comprehensible—order (see Briggs and Peat, 1989). The "new physics" affirms that we are inextricably linked to complex forces that are relatively inaccessible to conscious awareness. One task of analysis is to come to know, and to make known in verbal form, that which is communicated via other domains. As analysts, we align ourselves with the patterns of our patients' modes of being in the world: empathic attunement becomes a key to the world of the other. Reciprocally, our attempts toward attunement help our patients to incorporate rhythms of safety (Tustin, 1986) whereby they might better soothe (and thereby also come to know) self and other. In the reciprocal interactions of patient and analyst, meaning is both created and elucidated (Ogden, 1994), facilitating the transmission of shared understandings.

Matte-Blanco's (1975, 1988) work helps to elucidate that process of transmission, by pointing to the underlying reason inherent in that which we often term the "irrational." That term is often a euphemism for the unknown or ostensibly incomprehensible. Although we have many ways of "knowing" that have little to do with rational, verbal thought, we tend to underestimate the importance of attending to sensory information from other modalities. Many authors have pointed to the wealth of information that may be passed from one person to another without being elucidated in verbal form. Balint (1953), for example, noted the importance of enriching our understanding through the inclusion of other spheres, such as rhythmicity: a very basic form of pattern.

Nonverbal communications pose a special challenge, in that we don't have the comfort of the word to reassure us that we are in the right place at the right time. It would seem that when we are forced back into our bodies as primary receptor organs, we are uncomfortable to the extent that these organs have been unused and their data untested. How often we have been told—particularly as children, but also as adults—that we didn't really see what we thought we saw, hear what we heard, feel what we felt. This leads to a dual track of reality: an inner conviction, which is often hidden and thereby safeguarded, versus an outer conviction, which is largely public and mediated by our perceptions of consensual reality.

Our very training can impede our ability to comprehend. As Meltzer (1975) noted: "We have from our education and development a massive preconception of models and theories and ideas that we gradually have to get rid of in order to free ourselves to receive new impressions and to think new thoughts and entertain new models" (p. 289).

Bi-logic (Matte-Blanco, 1975, 1988) is one such model, which helps to elucidate both the formal structure underpinning our theories and also the processes at work within our selves and within the analytic hour, in the continuing interplay between the symmetrical and asymmetrical domains of being. Within the interworkings and interweavings of the analytic process, Simon was able to utilize the containing function enough to be able to experience sameness and yet to also make important distinctions between self and other, and between past, present, and future, which helped him to see and make sense of fundamental patterns organizing and constraining his experiences of self and other.

The analytic process is a paradoxical one, whereby growth is facilitated in much the same fashion as engendered by the koans of the Zen masters (Briggs and Peat, 1989). We journey into the irrational world in order to find meaning, which can only truly be held through its translation into the language of rational thought. And so, my patient journeys to another land to learn a new language, through which he might find the means to translate enough of his own history into his own words to find his own way. In this work, as we wander through lands of living metaphors, we would seem to need always to look forward in order to look backward, and to look backward in order to be able to see beyond.

3

AUTO-SENSUOUS SHAPES: PROTOTYPES FOR CREATIVE FORMS

*I*n this chapter, I highlight a type of patterned experience that has been referred to as "autistic" or "auto-sensuous" shapes by Tustin (1984, 1991) and others. Tustin (1984) described these as forms that are entirely idiosyncratic and personal, in which it is the bodily "feel" of the shape that matters most. Auto-sensuous shapes are depicted as presymbolic movements, a form of "unmentalized experience" (Mitrani, 1995) utilized toward self-soothing, which are often libidinally charged.[1] The original depiction of the concept came from the literature on autistic processes and has thereby become embedded in a pathological frame. However, there are also adaptive, normative, and creative aspects to these unconscious phantasies, founded in the early empathic attunement between infant and caregiver. Auto-sensuous shapes can be seen as transformations of basic sensory experience into creative endeavours, such as drawings, poetry, or the establishment of attunement and meaning-making within the analytic setting.

---

1. I am grateful to Judith Mitrani, whose explication of "autistic shapes" provided the inspiration for this chapter.

EARLY INFANT EXPERIENCE AND AUTO-SENSUOUS SHAPES

Early unconscious phantasy arises in the sensory experience of the infant, emerging from basic sensations of comfort and discomfort (Isaacs, 1948). These experiences give form, meaning, and coloration to all later understandings of self and world. The ability to be comfortable with both self and other depends on one's sense of capacity within the environment (Milner, 1952), derived from the early ability to evoke resonance from the mother.[2] The literature on autism delineates auto-sensuous shapes as one form of self-soothing at its pathological extreme, wherein the capacity for symbol formation has been diminished and we see largely its precursors (such as the autosensuous shapes that are not used to build understanding or communication, but rather take the place of these).

Optimally, the mother contains the anxiety of the child sufficiently to facilitate movements toward autonomous function. When separation occurs too soon, however, the illusion of union may evoke a sense of chaos, and separation may become a rigid need invoked to avoid that incipient sense of chaos (Milner, 1952). Babies who have not had sufficient "holding" (Winnicott, 1971) or "containment" (Bion, 1962, 1963) to facilitate the development of their own capacities for self-soothing and self-containment (Schore, 1994) may be missing what Tustin (1986) has referred to as the "rhythm of safety." Attempts toward self-soothing may then preclude the very type of dyadic experience that had been sought.

With no responsive mother to moderate affect at positive and negative ends to keep the infant from becoming overwhelmed, the infant is at the mercy of her own extremes of experience, caught between the Scylla of unbridled enjoyment and the Charybdis of unmitigated despair. There is most often no clear verbal narrative recording these early failures. Memories of very early experiences, occurring before the acquisition of language, become stored within the body and are expressed as

---

2. I am using "mother" in the generic sense of primary caretaker.

sensations rather than in more highly elaborated symbolic form (Innes-Smith, 1987). Therefore, as analysts, our understanding of these failures and their ramifications for individual development are often based on conjectures elaborated on sensations occasioned by our interactions, such as the constrictions experienced by our patients in their efforts to make meaning and derive enjoyment from their being-in-the-world.

The analyst attunes her self to the patient, much as the mother synchronizes her rhythms to those of her infant: this ability appears to be crucial for positive attachment (Stern, 1985; Anzieu, 1993). Our most primary experiences are of the body. As Freud (1923) noted, "the ego is first and foremost a bodily ego" (p. 26). Even before the caesura of birth, there are multiple months of experiences impinging themselves on the fetus's developing sensoria. Tustin (1969) described the infant's experience of being as a "stream of sensations." Alternatively, "in earliest days, the infant *is* the stream of sensations from which constructs gradually emerge as nameless entities. As some degree of separateness is tolerated, the infant may be said to interpret the world in terms of these nameless entities which are constellations of sensation" (Tustin, 1969, pp. 31–32).

According to Anzieu (1979, 1984, 1993), the earliest communications between infant and mother are of sound, rhythm, and of skin on skin, in which mother and infant are not yet differentiated: one is felt to be the "other side" of the other. This relationship is invoked as the child rubs self against self, imitating and thereby invoking this sense of merger of self with other. The infant's resources are limited, focused primarily on survival and secondarily on exploration of the environment, which is an important concomitant of survival, unless the external realities are intolerable (Fairbairn, 1952; Guntrip, 1989). In the absence of a good-enough environmental container, there arises a sense of emptiness—variously described as a "black hole" (Grotstein, 1991) or a terrible internal void that becomes fashioned in the image of the external one (Charles, 2000c). As one patient put it: "When I think of my childhood home, I think of her being there; she seems to be a part of it. But when I think of my childhood itself, I think of her being gone. She was never there."

At a very primary level, this absence may be experienced as an essential lack of containing function (which Bick [1968] termed a "psychic skin") on the part of certain infants. This psychic skin appears to be an essential foundation upon which notions of self and other can be built. Unmoderated affect overwhelms the child's defenses, breaking down the illusions of safety that help to contain experience and to bound self from other. Without these boundaries, the infant is unable to contain self or psychic contents, creating a terrible void in which neither ideas nor meaning can be held.

When the self cannot hold self, experience itself cannot be contained, leaving no ground on which to build (Winnicott, 1974; Eigen, 1998). Meaning seeps away (Anzieu, 1984), leading to fears of unintegration, seen as prior to and more primitive than fears of disintegration, echoing back to fears of being dependent in the face of an undependable other (Symington, 1985). At these times, human contact may represent the greatest danger. Symington (1985) suggested that the infant remediates this terror by focusing "attention on a sensory stimulus—visual, auditory, tactile, or olfactory. When his attention is held by this stimulus, he feels held together" (p. 481). He is also cut off, however, from the very type of engagement with an other that might ultimately provide hope for escape from this abyss.

PRIMARY EXPERIENCE AND AUTO-SENSUOUS SHAPES

The early months of life are crucial ones for the developing infant. Optimally, development brings greater levels of complexity and the biological and psychical become increasingly differentiated and integrated. In the absence of "good-enough" mothering, however, this process is impeded. Whether driven more primarily by infant need or environmental insufficiency, deficits may lead to an impaired ability to hold one's self within the world.

The mother, as container, moderates the child's experiences, optimally challenging the child just enough to facilitate the emerging capacity for self-holding and self-soothing. Disturbances in this emerging containing function may lead to deficits: the infant's receptivity becomes a danger to the extent that there is insufficient capacity to moderate incoming sensory experiences. An effective barrier then becomes the best course for survival. In the absence of a responsive external environment, patterned movement having to do with rhythmicity or tonus may represent attempts to supplement or sustain what is experienced as an inadequate "skin" or self-holding function (Mancia, 1981; Symington, 1985).

As an example, we might look at Symington's (1985) description of her observations of an infant in distress. The child's movements were at first chaotic and then became more intentional: clenching and unclenching her hands, arching her back, and pressing her hands and feet against the surface she was on. "This sequence of events illustrated repeated stresses for the baby being followed by attempts to hold herself together, at first by constant movement, and then by muscular tightening" (p. 482). The distress eased when the mother held the infant, and increased when the mother disrupted the infant's attempts to "hold" herself: "When the mother destroyed this holding by lifting the legs, the baby suddenly was no longer able to hold herself together and she spilled out from both her eyes and bladder" (p. 482).

As mentioned previously, many theorists have alluded to a primary state of being, sensation-dominated and presymbolic (Tustin, 1969; Ogden, 1989). This state is the domain of the unlinked bits of sensory experience that have been termed "beta-elements" by Bion (1962, 1967) and of the affectively charged phenomena described by Klein (1957) as preverbal "memories in feelings." These presymbolic mental phenomena may also take the form of the auto-sensuous shapes depicted by Tustin (1984). These primary experiences may be seen as forms of memory that are highly elusive to verbal representations and yet may contain important information as to how the psychic world is ordered and the external world understood.

Innes-Smith (1987) suggested that it is just at the point at which the child is beginning to organize body experiences toward the distinction of self and not-self that there is a propensity for "the formation of primary 'shapes' which offset the randomness of the flux of sensation which constitutes the infant's early sense of being" (p. 411). In the course of normal development, these primary shapes are confluences of sensation that, as they become related to the shapes of actual objects in the world, form the basis for object relations. The secure container appears to be essential for the process of separation, and with it the rudiments of meaning-making, to occur. Sufficient containment or moderation helps the child to make sense of and integrate his experiences. Without some titration, the child is at the mercy of overwhelming affect, which in itself is traumatic and must be defended against (Krystal, 1988). The consequent defenses tend to be quite primitive. At times, the sensation itself may become objectified and somewhat rigid, obstructing the child's ability to form meaningful relations with external objects.

Bick (1968) links the development of a "second skin" or false-self to this failure to integrate a sense of one's self as contained. The second skin is then utilized in the service of integrative and organizational processes toward the establishment of a more cohesive and coherent self. However, the individual may pay a high price for this adaptation in terms of fluidity and responsivity, developing a pseudo-independent false self with rigid defenses as substitutes for the more fluid containing function of the skin (Bick, 1968). For example, Bick described how a young girl would come into each session "hunched, stiff-jointed, grotesque like a 'sack of potatoes' as she later called herself" (p. 485). The girl was able to utilize the therapeutic interaction in the moment, but was not apparently able to sustain any improvements. "Utter dependence on the immediate contact could be seen and studied in the unintegrated states of posture and motility on the one hand, and thought and communication on the other, which existed at the beginning of each session, improving during the course, to reappear on leaving" (p. 485). In this way, self-definition seems to have remained a function of other, rather than of self.

External objects and parts of the self can be utilized toward the affirmation of self boundaries in other ways, as well, in the forms of repetitive touching, muscle tension, or skin rubbing against skin in a rhythmic fashion. Any of these can become the affirmation of containment in patterned (and therefore meaningful) forms—the rudiments of integrative processes. Depending on their further elaboration, or lack thereof, these processes may or may not become "meaningful" in the sense in which the term is most often used. Self-containing enactments such as these can remain unmentalized and preclude awareness, as would appear to be the case in autism. However, they also provide the rudiments of meaning: early experiences that are inaccessible to verbal memory may, at times, be accessed through the elaboration of this type of sensorimotor patterning—memories in feeling.

In line with observations by Freud (1900), Isaacs (1948), and others regarding the essential nature of the unconscious events or phantasies that underlie all mental processes, the developmental literature alludes to "generalized episodes" that are abstracted from specific occurrences and become prototypical expectations against which all later occurrences are gauged (Stern, 1985). This generalization—or pattern—becomes a meaningful structure that can be modified, further elaborated, or encapsulated, depending on the individual's later experiences and how and whether they can be integrated. Patterns may be extrapolated according to more or less complex sets of relationships. To the extent that the patterns are abstracted from the original experiences, they may be less accessible to consensual meanings. This characteristic is seen in primary process material, in which the symbols tend to be highly idiosyncratic. They are therefore best interpreted by the individual himself or herself until some other becomes familiar enough with these idiosyncratic patternings that their interpretations are more likely to be meaningful, as happens over time in analysis.

Narrative—or episodic—memory is an outgrowth of experience that is reliable enough that we are able to form and modify generalized conceptions in an ongoing fashion, wherein the sense of a "core" or cohesive self in relation to a coherent other is formed (Stern, 1985).

Many authors have described the "autistic"—or essentially self-focused—piece as an aspect of personality more generally, rather than being associated with some specific pathology or deficit (see Ogden, 1989). The capacity to take in sensory information at a very basic level, and to form impressions through the patternings of this data, is the foundation on which all later learning is built. Our basic equilibrium within the environment depends on our ability to take in sensory data and to order it in a coherent fashion—to "make sense" of it. However, intense fear tends to bring us back to basic survival issues, such as grounding ourselves in a sense of being. At this nonverbal level, efforts to recover from the type of freezing elicited by intense fear may initially focus on "bringing one's self back to life." Much as we might rub our hands to bring back the circulation in a frozen limb, we "rub" our surfaces more generally in attempts to soothe ourselves, using repetitive or rhythmic actions toward this end.

Primitive feelings of great need and dependency, in the face of fears that these will not be met, tend to elicit avoidant defenses on the surface. However, there will also be set in motion patterns of behavior, whether overt or covert, that will move toward soothing. Klein (1980) noted that these types of repetitive "autistic" phenomena also occur in "neurotic" adults, brought on by intense anxieties and fears of unintegration. These defenses may take on diverse forms. For example, words, themselves, may be used as a means of defense, rather than communication—to remain separate rather than to establish contact (Klein, 1980; Smith, 1990). Unlinking becomes the denial of meaning, which can be another use of these autosensuous shapes: in the circumscribed elaboration of form may lie either a search for, or a denial of, meaning.

DEVELOPMENT OF SYMBOLIC CAPACITY: THE IMPORTANCE OF ADEQUATE HOLDING OR CONTAINMENT

With the development of our symbolic functions, we tend to rely more heavily on language than on sensory experience in our conscious attempts to make sense of the world. Our more primary movements toward understanding shift to the background and become, to some extent, disowned. We are often surprised by nonverbal understandings and have developed rubrics, such as "insight" or "psychic powers" as putative explanatory mechanisms, which actually do little save to place the eminently comprehensible ostensibly beyond our comprehension. We "remember" the patterns built up through the impingements on our sensory apparatus, although they may be too complex to be comprehended fully in the moment.

The foundations for these patterns are built in early dyadic interactions in which the infant depends on the other for regulation of somatic and affective states. Experiences of overwhelming affect disrupt the child's developing capacities for self-regulation and meaning-making (Stern, 1985). Overwhelming affect inhibits the ability to scan for information and to thereby make sense of our experience. It is also important, however, to be able to remain isolated and detached from one's experiences in order to avoid becoming overwhelmed by the assaultive intrusion of the other (Grotstein, 1980). In addition to the self-containing and unifying functions of the protective skin, it also serves as a "stimulus barrier" (Krystal, 1988) that functions as a protective psychic barrier and also as a filter that makes symbolic representation possible (Anzieu, 1984). To this end, the autistic shape becomes a magic talisman by which this screen may be evoked and kept in place. As filter (Anzieu, 1984) or "beta-screen" (Bion, 1962), it provides one means for unlinking words and derealizing that which cannot be realized without overwhelming the resources of the self.

The screen has its own form, which comes to carry meaning, as do the multiple sensory elements absorbed by our senses. Gomberoff et al. (1990) suggested that prior to the consolidation of the separateness of self and other, the forerunners of mental representations "become imprinted in the organism . . . forming very primitive mosaics, which have been conceptualized as autistic, of primitive or primary identification" (p. 249). Autosensuous shapes may also be seen as precursors of transitional objects "based on tactile sensations of continuity" (Gaddini, 1987, p. 324). Gaddini suggested that the loss of the precursor is tantamount to the loss of self, as there is as yet insufficient organization to allow mourning. One might imagine that the search for soothing becomes a search for the "me," in the presence of the "not-me" that evokes annihilation/abandonment anxieties. The need for contact—such as may be seen in autistic shapes, thumb-sucking, or other autosensual experience—becomes a search for some means for containing the sense of self (Gaddini, 1987). The utilization of form can provide one mode of relief in this ongoing search for soothing.

The multimodal nature of experience expands the potentialities for achieving self-soothing. Equivalence implies reflexivity, symmetry, and transitivity, which is not the same as identity (Matte-Blanco, 1975). It is, rather, a more highly elaborated function of being able to transpose essential elements of meaning from one experience to another. In this way, it involves the ability to discriminate both sameness and difference and to recognize cross-modal equivalencies, abilities that appear to be present from infancy (Stern, 1985). For example, infants show a great sensitivity to temporal aspects of their environment and are able to translate these patterns from the visual to the auditory and vice versa. Infants appear to abstract categories from their experience, which they then use toward making discriminations in, and thereby making sense of, their environment. We rely on patterns to note essential meanings across domains.

Stern (1985) noted the dynamic aspects of affect that describe the pattern and trajectory of the experience. His notion of activation contour is particularly useful in attempts to understand auto-sensuous shapes. My sense is that these shapes become a concrete representation of an activation contour, such as self-soothing. Optimally, the human face and form become associated with the onset of soothing regulatory functions. However, in the absence of this important link, the human face and form may provide a need for defensive self-soothing in the face of what have become anxiety-producing stimuli. The emotionally present mother, absent, may be invoked as a soothing presence derived from self/other experience, whereas the emotionally absent mother, present, requires an alternative source of soothing.[3] The child's ability to manipulate flesh on flesh in rhythmic form becomes an opportunity for self-soothing in just this way.

Tustin (1991) described autism as "a massive 'not-knowing' and 'not-hearing' provoked by traumatic awareness of body separateness" (p. 586), in the service of survival. The creative endeavor may become a container for this intolerable awareness of separateness, in the form of protective autogenerated shapes, with their calming or soothing effects. Tustin (1991) described these auto-sensuous shapes as "endogenous swirls of sensation [that] . . . distract attention from unbearable bodily separateness, and assuage the terrors" (p. 588), but also become a form of prison, as entrenched modes of behavior that cut the child off from other experiences. It is also, however, a creative act. When communicated in some form that can be received by an other, it becomes a link to the other and thereby to meaning— a consensual symbol.

SYMBOL FORMATION

Segal (1957) suggested that symbol formation is a function of self-soothing. We derive symbols as a means for dealing with anxieties associated with our object relations, primarily the fear of the bad object and the fear of the loss of the good object. As aspects of self are projected into and become identified with the object or external world, the part that contains the internal object becomes identified with and serves to represent the inter-

3. I am grateful to James Grotstein for making this important distinction.

nal object. "These first projections and identifications are the beginning of the process of symbol formation" (Segal, 1957, p. 393). In the earliest stages of development, symbols are not experienced as symbol, but as object. Klein (1930) termed these "symbolic equations," in that no distinction is made between the symbol and that which is symbolized: the two are one. "In the symbolic equation, the symbol-substitute is felt to *be* the original object. The substitute's own properties are not recognized or admitted. The symbolic equation is used to deny the absence of the ideal object, or to control a persecuting one" (Segal, 1957, p. 395).

With the establishment of the good object, the use of symbols changes. In particular, as empathy develops, so does the need to inhibit libidinal and aggressive aims. The symbol provides an important means for displacing aggression and lessening fears of loss (Segal, 1957). The internalization of the symbol becomes "a means of restoring, re-creating, recapturing and owning again the original object. But in keeping with the increased reality sense, they are now felt as created by the ego and therefore never completely equated with the original object" (Segal, 1957, p. 394).

The distinction between symbol and object serves important developmental and integrative functions. Symbol formation becomes a means whereby we "can be consciously aware and in control of *symbolic expressions* of the underlying primitive phantasies" (Segal, 1957, p. 396). This provides a basis for self and other communication: "Not all internal communication is verbal thinking, but all verbal thinking is an internal communication by means of symbols–words" (p. 396). To the extent that a symbol is distinguished from the original object, it becomes a creation of the subject and may thereby be more freely utilized. Whereas consensual symbols become tools for reciprocal communication between self and other, idiosyncratic symbols may become tools for defensive exclusion of the other.

There is a privacy inherent in the formation of autistic shapes. The elaboration of a sense of continuity (meaning) in the presence of the other becomes the reassurance that the self can be sustained in the presence of the other. Integral to the understanding of the roots of this experience is the awareness of the extent and nature of the fears at this level of experience, "such as the unconscious anxiety that aspects of oneself are so private and so central to an endangered sense of being alive that the very act of communication will endanger the integrity of the self" (Ogden, 1989, p. 15). From this perspective, the act of creation becomes the encoded tentative interpolation of the self toward the other, in a fashion sufficiently cryptic that one might retreat, ostensibly unharmed, and yet containing enough of the essence of the self that one might, indeed, be "seen."

FORM: AN ESSENTIAL ASPECT OF THE CREATIVE ACT

Form is defined variously in the *Concise Oxford Dictionary* as: (1 a) a shape; an arrangement of parts. (b) the outward aspect (esp. apart from colour) or shape of a body . . . (3) the mode in which a thing exists or manifests itself . . . (9) a set order . . . a formula . . . (16) arrangement and style in literary or musical composition . . . (17) Philos. the essential nature of a species or thing.

In his psychoanalytic exposition of aesthetic form as an "organizing unity," Rose (1980) suggested that "all other principles of aesthetic form, such as thematic variation, balance, development, and intensity, are subsidiary to organic unity" (p. 4). From this frame, order and rhythmicity may be seen as essential facets of form. This definition affirms the essential, universal quality of basic structure, as well as the particular manifestations or derivations of that basic form.

Rose (1980) depicted the essential dialectic of the creative process as one between the ambiguity of primary process and the control of secondary process; between physical events and semantic meaning; and between infinite variety and oneness. The creative endeavor becomes an attempt to capture some facet of this variety in a manner that brings the onlooker closer to the essential form that underlies it. In this way, the particular is seen as a manifestation of a greater whole. This view is highly consistent with the Freudian view of overdetermination, in that essential aspects of experience will be represented in great multiplicity, making more likely their eventual recognition. We can find many other examples of this type of phenomena, for example in the so-called "repetition compulsion," wherein that which is not worked through becomes a dilemma with which we face ourselves in successive iterations, over and over again.

There are many rhythms to the human experience, some of which appear to be essential and universal. Notable among these are various forms of soothing, such as rocking or sucking. Individual variations may be recognizable variants on these universal themes, or may be so idiosyncratic as to be virtually unrecognizable without reference to the contexts in which they have arisen. As examples of the latter, we may think of headbanging, or the cutting or burning that, for some of our patients, become forms of self-soothing. Rose (1980) noted that the "new physics" asserts the importance of an understanding of form over content, in a universe that is not static, but ever changing, wherein "the properties of material things are understandable only in terms of their interaction with the rest of the world with which they are always engaged" (p. 23). Rather than becoming overwhelmed by the multiplicity inherent in this view, we may turn to the soothing certainty of form, in which inheres an unchanging essence within its myriad manifestations. It is rather like a dream, in which we may have a dazzling array of apparently diffuse elements all leading us back to some rather simple dilemma requiring our attention.

For some individuals, it becomes imperative to create of these essential dilemmas an elaborate display in order to obscure the essential vulnerability underlying them. We can see, in many creative endeavors, a repetitive engagement with a troubling—or soothing—theme. These bodies of work bear the imprint of patterns being continually elaborated in repeated attempts at self-soothing, communication, and working through. For example, I work with one writer whose novels are highly diverse in their outer manifestations of time and place, and yet the interactions of the characters may be seen as an evolving interplay, over time, of the same configurations that troubled him in childhood and permeate his analytic material, as well. His troubled sleep and waking dreams provide continuing opportunities to enact, discharge, and play with the ongoing threats of abandonment and annihilation that enliven the landscapes of his productions, at one step removed from the infinitely more terrifying world of actual people.

Symbolic functions enable us to play with that which might be too terrifying if it were to be perceived as too real. The dialectic between physical events and semantic meaning gives art a plasticity that provokes growth (Rose, 1980), much as does paradox: it is in the nature of metaphor to expand meaning and to heighten our appreciation of "reality." The interplay of the familiar and unfamiliar promotes growth, and also enhances our ability to perceive the underlying structure or meaning. Before content there is form, as evidenced by the child's delight in the production of speech: "In the beginning babbling is probably a direct expression of libidinal satisfaction without symbolic referents" (Rose, 1980, p. 139).

Rhythmicity contains the dialectic of recurrence and change. Growth is a function of change within the order—of surprise. Within the ongoing flow of sameness lies the soothing function, which enables us to tolerate the novel, to attend to it, and to move toward it in attempts at integration. Whether framed in terms of inside versus outside, self versus other, or conscious versus unconscious, this is the primary dialectic in which all growth occurs. The affirmation and elaboration of both sameness and difference are the essential roots of meaning (Matte-Blanco, 1975), establishing equivalencies in the refinding of the self in the other and thereby delimiting the bounds of reality (Freud, 1925).

SYMBOLS AND CREATIVITY

Sameness and difference become building blocks for understanding, foundational for the processes of generalization and abstraction. Within the dialectic created by these basic processes comes the basis for symbol formation, a precondition of both creativity and understanding. Milner (1952) suggested that the drive toward making meaning wells from an "internal necessity for inner organization, pattern, coherence, the basic need to discover identity in difference without which experience becomes chaos" (p. 84). Chaos, to some extent, is a function of two-dimensional space—or, in Grotstein's (2000b) terms, "infinite" or "null" space—space that has not yet been ordered and therefore cannot be thought about. Without the advantage of greater perspective, there is no possibility of identificatory process, only rote imitation, with an associated emotional shallowness and lack of meaning. Meltzer (1975) noted that autistic patients, as they get better, describe their experience as one of chaos, from which growth ensues through the ordering of the chaos into meaningful elements that may be further elaborated over time.

This ability to distinguish between elements is essential for the elaboration of symbols in formal, asymmetrical thinking. Anticipating Matte-Blanco (1975), Milner (1952) suggested that finding new objects entails the ability to discover the familiar in the unfamiliar, which requires "an ability to tolerate a temporary loss of sense of self, a temporary giving up of the discriminating ego which stands apart and tries to see things objectively and rationally and without emotional colouring" (p. 97). She likened this temporary loss of self to the "aesthetic moment," in which one "loses one's self" in the process of becoming absorbed by the work of art. This absent presence is both a part of the creative act and a mode whereby it can be deeply appreciated. It is also an essential element of the analytic enterprise, in which we become lost in the process and yet maintain an observing ego through which to make sense of our experiences.

Milner (1957) equated creativity with symbol formation, whether it is feeling or knowing that is being symbolized. Although the sense of union, merger, or "oceanic feeling" is often represented as a regressive return to the womb or breast, Milner (1957) suggested that this immersion into primary unity may also provide a means for redifferentiation of self and other in novel fashion, a necessary prerequisite for creative activity. This sense of union may represent, not a yearning for dependent reliance on the other, but rather a very fundamental return to the self as source. The "inherent rhythmic capacity of the psycho-physical organism can become a source of order that is more stable than reliance on an order imposed either from outside, or by the planning conscious mind" (Milner, 1957, p. 224). There may be a regressive feel to these primary rhythms, but that may be an artifact of dicta that proscribe and constrain our experience through the imposition of social values.

The roots of creativity are derived in our early experiences of self and other, self within other, and other within self. Much as the earliest transformative experiences occur through the reverie of the mother, later creative acts require the internal capacity for reverie, made possible by a setting in which we are freed, for some time, of the necessity for vigilance (Milner, 1957). The mother's reverie and attunement become prototypes for our own ability to be with our selves and to let go of any rigid distinctions between self and other. In those moments, settled within our own rhythms, we are more free to respond to them as they strike us. Perhaps it is in those odd moments of relatively unconstrained thinking that internal form can best become symbolized. That would certainly seem to be the principle underlying many aspects of the analytic setting.

Milner's (1956) depictions of the creative process spring from a deep desire to understand both self and other. She described art as a union of "feminine" and "masculine" elements: the infinitely receptive aspect versus that which actively constrains into known modes or patterns. She noted that this dialectic is similar to the process of analysis, in which there is an interplay between the receptive "free associations" and the constraints of theoretical forms. Creativity requires the relatively free interplay of phantasy and thinking; symmetry and asymmetry; unconscious and conscious processes. Most fundamentally, art is a personal process, derived from moments of being.

A work of art, whatever its content, or subject, whether a recognizable scene or object or abstract pattern, must be an externalization, through its shapes and lines and colours, of the unique psycho-physical rhythm of the person making it. Otherwise it will have no life in it whatever, for there is no other source for its life [Milner, 1957, p. 230].

This quality of absorption is essential in regard to the medium as well: for Milner, the relationship between the artist and her medium of expression is one of union, of knowing the other enough to both know it as other and to also be totally present within it—a cogent description of our task as analysts.

Milner (1957) noted the importance in art of being able to create symbols for the expression of the inner life. Speaking specifically of the visual arts, she suggested that

since this inner life is the life of a body, with all its complexities of rhythms, tensions, releases, movement, balance, and taking up room in space, so surely the essential thing about the symbols is that they should show in themselves, through their formal pattern, a similar theme of structural tensions and balances and release, but transfigured into a timeless visual co-existence [p. 226].

The primary function of art may be the creation of new objects, rather than the restoration of lost ones (Milner, 1957). It is in the novel putting together of unlike things in unlikely ways that we begin to see anew that which we had come to not-see, by force of habit or prohibition (Symington, 1983; Charles, 1998). This synthesis is done by

unmasking old symbols and making new ones, thus incidentally making it possible for us to see that the old symbol was a symbol; whereas before we had thought the symbol was a "reality" because we had nothing to compare it with: in this sense . . . continually destroying "nature" and re-creating nature [Milner, 1957, p. 229].

AUTO-SENSUOUS SHAPES AND THE ARTISTIC PROCESS

The artistic process is one whereby what Bollas (1987) referred to as the "unthought known" can be formally represented and thereby known. What is fundamentally self becomes externalized, whereby it becomes more than self and more than other, thereby potentially taking on some aspect of the universal. This universality gives art its enduring appeal and provides the experienced sense of moving toward "truth" or "O" ("Ultimate Reality"; Bion, 1965). Formalization implies creating a structure. The creative endeavor is most effective when it allows us to move between the levels of conscious and unconscious, in the forms of sensory experience, fragmentation, and meaning (integration)[4], without fear of becoming trapped in one or—alternatively and perhaps most profoundly—when we can experience all three simultaneously. Although they are often discussed as discrete or dichotomous and thereby pathologized, especially at the more "primitive" levels, these three modes of being also represent profound resources for creativity. It is no wonder that people confuse creativity and madness: creativity takes us to the brink, and it can be a terrifying and yet awesome (awe-ful?) view.

As we approach the simultaneity of the three modes of being, we move closer to the realm of metaphor. Arlow (1979) suggested that "metaphor can be understood in a more general way as a fundamental aspect of how human thought integrates experience and organizes reality" (p. 368). The term is derived from the Greek, "to transfer," implying a transference of meaning from one thing to another. Figurative language involves the saying of one thing with the intention of meaning another to achieve a novel meaning that may be either wider or more precise than the original meaning. The metaphoric relationship creates a distance between the reality referred to and the mode of expression, making it easier to think about each, as well as about the relationship between the two. In this way, it introduces

---

4. corresponding roughly to the autistic-contiguous, paranoid-schizoid, and depressive positions.

the transitional space (Winnicott, 1953) and facilitates creativity, as in the ability to play with an idea (Winnicott, 1971).

When I first read Mitrani's (1995) explication of autistic shapes, I thought of my own experiences with patterned forms or sensations that become the impetus for the expression of complex and often relatively unconscious affects. For me, these forms become vehicles for the transmission of meaning in many ways. They become elaborated in black ink on white paper as relatively simple, repetitive patterns, which accrue into complex representations of sensations that had eluded verbal expression. Quite profoundly, my hand comes to know the subtleties of the endeavor in ways my conscious mind cannot apprehend, as my hand learns to feel the nuance of form that will give representation to distance, dimensionality, rhythm, and texture. The drawing process, itself, takes the form of absorption into the patterned detail, alternating with movements far enough away from the detail to be able to grasp the representation as a whole. It is in the interplay of sensory experience, detail, and gestalt that form is represented as both underlying and overarching structure, and takes on a depth and multiplicity of meaning hitherto unimagined.

My poems, as well, often begin with intense sensation that eludes representation in verbal expression, but rather comes to me as a rush of patterned elements, much as depicted by Stern (1985) as "affective contours"—sensory melodies, using words as the "structural invariants" (Cooper and Aslin, 1994). There is an associative element that works at many levels simultaneously, joining image to image, sound to sound, meaning to meaning. As in my drawings, the depth and the multiplicity of meaning in the patternings of these elements often eludes me until the sequence has run its course, and the words stare back at me from the printed page, awaiting elaboration or refinement. Once again, there is the interplay between the elements themselves; their interrelationships within the structure; and the larger structure as a whole, which becomes more than I could have imagined. In this way, the creative act is born out of the basic patterns of meaning imprinted on us by our experience, but not yet "known." Through the medium of choice, these patterns become elaborated into concrete symbols, which can then be manipulated by the conscious mind into patterns that make sense at that level, as well. This is not so different from the processes at work in that other art cum science: psychoanalysis.

AUTO-SENSUOUS SHAPES AND THE PSYCHOANALYTIC PROCESS

Bianchedi (1991) suggested that "mental growth will consist in 'making the unthought thinkable'" (p. 11). It entails a continuing process of making manifest that which has remained as background, eluding our attention and verbal understanding. The analytic process is furthered to the extent that we can translate ostensibly meaningless interactions with patients into patterned and meaningful material. To this end, containment may be a necessary prerequisite for rendering the unknown known (Mitrani, 1995). Empathic attunement involves the "ability to be influenced by the form, sequence, and context and patterning" (Arlow, 1979, p. 373) and to be stimulated by whatever message might be contained therein, even when the receiver is not consciously aware of the contents of the message itself. These unique configurations become purveyors of meaning beyond any conscious awareness. Over time, through the patternings of an individual's displays, we may come to infer important themes that have shaped his or her experiences and their products.

Psychic growth has been postulated as the ultimate aim of analysis: "the interpretation should be such that the transition from knowing about reality to becoming real is furthered" (Bion, 1965, p. 153). This transition "is of particular concern to the analyst in his function of aiding maturation of the personalities of patients" (Bion, 1965, p. 158). In spite of our best intentions, however, we often tend to avoid knowledge that seems too painful. Psychological phenomena, in particular, are easy to avoid, as they are not amenable to apprehension by the senses (Bion, 1965). Evasive efforts may precipitate movements toward the concrete, often in the form of bodily discomforts that become the ostensible source of the pain—a focus on sensation rather than sentiment (McDougall, 1974).

Bion (1965) noted our terror in the face of "the unknowable and hence of the unconscious in the sense of the undiscovered or the unevolved" (p. 171), suggesting that our only hope for real transformation lies in our ability to abstract from our experience, thereby avoiding the obfuscating effects of the concrete and particular. However, "confronted with the unknown, 'the void and formless infinite,' the personality of whatever age fills the void (saturates the element), provides a form (names and binds a constant conjunction) and gives boundaries to the infinite (number and position)" (Bion, 1965, p. 171). We are always caught between our desire to understand and the tremendous difficulties we encounter in our attempts to contemplate, in spite of our terror, the unknown (Charles, 1999b, 2001d).

In our work, there is often a sensory experience of pattern, either affective or somatic, that becomes a cue or signal. We have caught some pattern or theme in our unconscious register, which resonates in some familiar—or unfamiliar—manner, thereby inviting our attention. We tend to talk about these resonances globally, as "tuning the unconscious" to that of the other. This type of global statement overlooks important questions as to the nature of the instrument being tuned or the medium of attunement. Rayner (1992) has noted that the analytic enterprise is built on empathic attunement to preverbal events: it is through the emotional resonance, or matching, of the patient's rhythms or patterns that primary meanings become elucidated.

In my experience, there are often swirls of sensation (much as described by Tustin, 1991) that have a familiar feel, suggesting an oblique pattern that seems to carry thematic meaning in relation to the patient's material. Alternatively, the form may feel quite static, like the haunting, yet elusive, residual sense of space in the wake of a particularly evocative dream. Often these experiences are cross-modal in nature. The form, as experienced, bears no overt resemblance to that to which I am relating it, but carries the same essential pattern. The pattern may bear the form of an affective contour or sensory melody that carries its own meaning, if I can only be receptive enough to discover it. It is very much like the use of symbols in dreams, for example, in which we may "know" the identity of a person in spite of any ostensible dissimilarities. We often have the sense of very strongly knowing the pattern without being able to give a name to it.

Attempts to articulate or communicate this function are elusive, similar to the fate that has befallen projective identification. Our attempts to communicate often obscure the subtleties of the processes themselves. In the moment, however, we become aware of some presence that carries meaning. This may come in the form of an idea or sensation, or fragment of dream or memory that ostensibly, on the surface, does not "fit." It is like a recurrent shadow that haunts us by virtue of its elusive familiarity. We both know it and not-know it simultaneously, as though registering the perception in the wrong key. At these times, if I can catch the thought or sensation or fragment and attend to the form of it, to the underlying inchoate "meaning" of it, my thoughts often lead in a more fruitful direction than if I were to impose meaning by rational order.

Perhaps these are the times when the unconscious may become conscious: we enter into the profound and uncanny twilit world of the preconscious, in which there is greater accessibility to nonverbal knowings. I would contend that one profound entry into this world is through the vehicle of form, by which we can leap from equivalence to equivalence through the shortcut path of what Freud (1915) called "primary process" and Matte-Blanco (1975) referred to as "symmetrization." In these moments, when our capacity to make meaning at an unconscious level greatly exceeds our capacity to understand from a conscious perspective, form may be the key.

For example, there are times of boredom or distress in which I find myself making patterned movements between forefinger and thumb. Often these take the form of circular, repetitive shapings. However, there are also moments when I find myself detailing a more complex pattern, at times in the form of an elaboration of a letter of the alphabet. There is an order to these shapings: in some ways it has the feel of a repetitive or compulsive act. As with any repetitive act, however, at some level there is meaning in the choice of this act over some other and I wonder about the choice of this particular movement, this particular pattern, at this particular time. At times, I notice my patient moving in reciprocal rhythms and wonder whether my self-soothing has become their own. If so, does it further the process by enabling them to tolerate the awfulness, or short-circuit it by immolating their fear in some safe, but distant, shroud? Alternatively, I also wonder how my movements become informed by their own. This interplay would seem to be part of the dance, as we communicate meanings through our bodies that our conscious minds cannot yet comprehend.

CASE ILLUSTRATION

The *Concise Oxford Dictionary* defines the artist's medium as "the intervening substance through which impressions are conveyed to the senses." From this framework, the analyst's medium is her self: from basic sensory experience, through the whole range of affective experiences and contours, through her history of dreaming and waking life, to the theories and other abstractions that gird, order, and give meaning to it. As I sat in session with one patient in particular, a writer for whom the interpersonal world has been very treacherous, I noticed her hands moving within one another. In the moment, I became aware of my own thumb and forefinger moving in resonance to the rhythm of my patient's hands. I could not tell whose movements had preceded whose, but I did notice over the course of the session that the reciprocal movements became slower as the work deepened.

"Nina" asked about my rug: had I reversed it? It could have been another rug she was thinking of, she said. I reminded her of a dream in which the rug had become huge and was hanging on the wall. "I remember," she said, her face softening like an Italian Madonna at my memory of her memory. "It was black, and the same pattern was in the floor." The effect had been overwhelming to her, much as I become too large and treacherous as she comes to rely on me. She began to talk more freely and then caught herself; "I forgot to listen to myself," she said. "It's always hard to know if one is safe," I replied. "I just like to keep track," she said. "But then, that changes the track," I responded. "Yes," she nodded, "It does."

"I dread coming here," she said, after a pause, "but then, there's the promise. I *have* been feeling better. At work, when I get anxious, I can calm myself down. When it's bad, I don't try to do the numbers in my head and I slow down and take deep breaths and it's OK."

Nina told me about work: the people who had bothered her so intensely are bothering her less. Her "nemesis" was in the store one day and it became apparent that the woman was not really actively evil, just miserable. An older couple came in, immersed in their own private bubble. They were rude and condescending and seemed to have no idea there were actual people there with whom they were interacting. My patient is tired of being unreal to others: her mother lives in a fantasy in which Nina is just an "extra," and yet her mother wants her always on stage to play against. She is like a prop, admonished to have no needs of her own.

"Perhaps," I said, "the attacks now are a lot like the food fights when you were a kid. You got in the way of the food: it wasn't necessarily directed at you. And yet, the attacks have always felt personal, as though they were about you. But then, in that moment at work, you saw the vulnerability behind the assault—that horrible woman trying in such pathetic ways to be part of things. I think that that couple must have felt very much like your parents to you, using you as a prop, but dehumanizing you in the process. All these people, lost in their own fantasies, not really able to be present in the moment." Nina was silent for a while. "I'm holding on to what you said," she said, "so I can think about it." "Perhaps it was too much?" I wondered. "No," she said, "I just want to be able to hold on to it."

In a subsequent hour, Nina told me of a horror story she had been reading: "It's about a psychologist who murders people and blames his patient. The patient is put to death, but manages to not die, becoming the undead and bringing others back to life. It's not the story I'm thinking of, it's the scene; this cemetery; it is so vivid and the characters keep chasing through it for one reason or another. That author," she said, smiling, after a pause; "he is so good, he hooks you in the first paragraph; it's so vivid." I wondered silently about how she becomes responsible for my killing her, and how confusing it all becomes to her, and how she keeps herself safe by staying outside.

At times, I can find her; I can move within her rhythms. As her words create images, I can sense meaning and put it into words that interplay with her own. However, my overall experience of being with Nina, particularly at the beginning of each hour, is rather chaotic. She comes in disjointed: she had either dreaded coming or, alternatively, had looked forward to the session but then had been shaken by the harshness of the disjunction of anticipation meeting reality. It is like the story she described, in which there is a sense of vitality that engages her, but along with it comes the chaos and the terror. The process here, too, is jumbled. As I write notes in retrospect, I create order from the seemingly disparate fragments, which nevertheless weave together into meaningful forms.

In one particularly fragmented hour, occasioned by having spent the previous afternoon with her mother, Nina described her mother as a loosely running monologue, relatively impervious to Nina's interpolations. Nina is embarrassed by her mother's vacuity and her symmetrizations of self and daughter—most notably her assumptions that Nina believes in the "new age" phenomena to which her mother adheres. Nina recalls how, as a child, she tried hopelessly to follow her mother's explications of the latest rite or ritual that had caught the mother's attention, always accompanied by her mother's disdainful assumption that Nina would inevitably fail to comprehend the meaning or value of this particular endeavor. In this way, her mother created of her a vacant audience, until Nina had little assurance of her own existence in any positive sense.

At times I find Nina's associations difficult to follow. I have the sense that she both longs to be understood and is terrified of that very understanding, as though she might be annihilated by it. During the session I have been describing, there was one segment that I found to be particularly labyrinthian. I was uncertain as to whether there was some defect in my attention or whether her thoughts were as fragmented as they seemed. The words seemed to have meaning on the face of them, but the face was only a tiny indication of the meaning, much like seeing a speck on the surface of dark water, and having the sense of a mammoth iceberg spreading its bulk below. I could recall that she had been talking about a space, which was a wound—terribly vulnerable and needing to be protected—and how she would become aware of it in the company of others and feel very visible and at risk, and how her internal preoccupations would become so compelling that she found it difficult to attend to whatever was actually happening in the room.

Nina then said that she often finds herself not really paying attention to what people are saying, but rather finds herself running through her own thoughts, reserving just enough to scan the external conversation. This was a very vivid image for me, particularly striking in light of the symmetry with my own experience of finding myself processing internally and letting her words run by. I wondered silently whether this was a comment on her perception of having been left alone in the moment. When Nina said that she wonders if that is what makes it difficult for her to be around people, I wondered silently about this allusion—was it perhaps a justification for not wanting to be around people, or a reference to the actual experience of finding it difficult to actually be with or make contact with another person. She then said, "I don't know what I mean." I said that I wondered if she said that when she was aware of a diversity of meanings and was feeling vulnerable and fearful, not knowing what meaning the other person might be making and fearing she would be uncomfortable with their construal. She looked at me with greater attention. "Yes," she said. "But *you* must be aware of the different meanings."

In that moment, I sensed Nina's fear that I might be omniscient, which seemed to be equated with seeing whatever meaning seemed most awful at the moment. In this way, I seemed to become her father, defining her as "bad" for having her own needs or ideas in opposition to those of her mother. I said that I might be aware of some diversity of meanings, but would inevitably miss others. I didn't want to destroy this mutual coming toward knowing by some belief in my knowing in the face of her not-knowing. I struggled to find words and to also keep the point. I found it exceedingly difficult and had to begin speaking without knowing, in order to be able to even move toward knowing. All I had to go on, at the moment, was the form that the awareness had taken within my sensoria. There were no words.

Struggling toward words in that moment required a great deal of faith on my part, which was tenuous, and yet I persisted, hoping that the words might emerge as I groped toward them, holding the form that seemed to underlie them in my mind. I began to speak from the form itself, telling her that when she had been describing that experience of having two tracks going on, an interior one based on her own preoccupations and another one that was concerned with tracking the external rhetoric, and had then said something about wondering if that was why she found it difficult to be around people, I had not known exactly what she had meant. I had given her the two threads that had come to my mind and yet there might also be others. I said that it had appeared to me that she was struggling with that same diversity of meanings, which was what had elicited my comment. Nina seemed to "get it"—that we were both grappling with conceptions that are difficult to understand and make sense of, much less articulate, but that nevertheless seemed important enough to me to make that attempt, in spite of the difficulty.

I said that it made sense that she would need to keep one track open in that way, her childhood experience having been one of having her mother's ongoing verbiage continually assaulting her. Much of it must have been incomprehensible to her as a child and yet she had had to keep it organized in some fashion, in order to protect herself. And so, she had learned to attend to certain cues that necessitated certain actions on her part, without really attending to the ongoing discourse in any integrative or ostensibly meaningful fashion. I suggested that her early experience of living in a household in which her mother's highly idiosyncratic reality was the only important one had made it difficult for Nina to maintain herself in the face of opposition to her opinions. With some grounding from early childhood to support us, we can better tolerate those types of assaults to the self. However, for Nina there had been insufficient grounding assurance of the sturdiness of her self.

"What do I do with this?" Nina asked. "You're not going to tell me," she answered herself. "I don't have the audacity to assume that I could know," I replied. "You will do what you will do and you will come back and we'll see where you've gone and we'll try to understand. That's all we can do. The more you can bring in your own metaphors and experiences and let me inside of them as you have done today, the better I will be able to understand you from your own frame of reference, so that I might actually be able to be helpful. But that is difficult, because it means getting past the line you were talking about, about needing to keep the interior safe."

Nina was silent for a few minutes, then glanced toward the window, from which vantage point she could see the clock. I sensed that the time was oppressing her, and waited. She said that she had a lot to think about, and left. There was a comfort in her leaving, which I took as an auspicious sign.

In this interaction, my sense was that both Nina and I were struggling with preconscious forms that were difficult to elaborate into words: this transformation depended on faith in both self and other. The process of becoming attuned to one another seems to have provided the context in which this faith might flourish, in spite of her terror at being known/devoured/devouring. This symmetrization may be seen as a fundamental confusion, patterned on her experiences of being with her mother, with whom survival depended on remaining fundamentally unknown. Any act of self-assertion was perceived as a threat to the mother, which was also a threat to the relationship and thereby to Nina's very being.

One of the forms that Nina and I create between us is that of the space itself. We begin disjointed, fragmented, and then by the end of the hour, there is the palpable sense of circular form surrounding us, as though we had created, once more, a womb within which to sustain ourselves. For Nina, a gifted musician, this container seems to be patterned in the musical notes and scores within which she soothes herself. Her idioms are not my own, and yet they seem to find corresponding metaphors within the sensations and images evoked within me during our times together.

Nina had lived her whole life in a world in which there was no responsive other to attend to her, without paying some terrible price. She had become reclusive and had patterned herself to the music she loves, the authors who seemed to really "see," or the cats who were reliably open and beyond deceit. There was a whole world of beauty she treasured and tried to safeguard in the face of the horror that people had become for her. She came in to see me with huge trepidations, fearing imminent destruction as the patternings of my universe threatened to overpower her attempts to attend to and begin to order the rhythms of her own.

Nina's "rhythms of safety" had become solitary ones, by which she ensured that safety, but also entombed herself. Her intense vulnerability had been such that she remained ever vigilant for signs that I, too, was one of the walking dead, silently eating her alive or, alternatively, that she might annihilate me through her terrible, devouring need. And yet, she came. "There's the promise," she says. There's the hope of being held and not being dropped precipitously, I think. There's the unthought hope of coming to hold herself lovingly, without this terror and awful isolation.

CONCLUSION

At times our work is like separating the layers of a palimpsest to reveal their multiplicity, each reflecting a different, yet convergent, meaning. As with a fine gem, the whole is always more than the sum of the parts, the placement of each facet revealing the core in a new and unique way. For Nina, the core is unknowable, too fraught with terror to see directly without feeling as though she would be annihilated by the sight. And so we look indirectly as we register our experiences of being with one another, and struggle to make meaning through our elaborations of those experiences. The analytic enterprise is often like a hall of mirrors, in which we can never quite see directly that which we are attempting to observe. As we walk through these halls of mirrors, our sensory experience can become our greatest ally in recognizing and elaborating the essential rhythms of self and other, thereby promoting the further conception and real-ization of the self.

4

NONPHYSICAL TOUCH: MODES OF CONTAINMENT AND COMMUNICATION WITHIN THE ANALYTIC PROCESS

I once interpreted to a patient that he had not felt "held" in his object world: his mother had been unable to hold him in such a way that he might have felt safe and soothed. Later, as he talked disdainfully about this notion of mine that his mother had not "held him properly," I realized how profoundly he had not heard what I had intended to say. In that moment, I was aware of the enormous gulf that existed between us. Although I could resonate to the experience of the child who had been held neither safely nor sufficiently, I was unable to communicate this resonance in a way that did not recapitulate the original failure. He could be held neither safely nor sufficiently by my words. My reflections on this interactive failure have led me to think more specifically about analytic notions of holding and being held, and of how we touch one another and are touched in this most intimate of environments in which physical touch is so greatly constrained.

Psychoanalysis has been, from its inception, preoccupied with issues of touching and being touched, holding and being held. Freud seems to have been very aware of the power of contact, first using hypnosis to "take hold" of the mind of the other and then using his hands to bring thoughts forward through the power of his touch (Breuer and Freud, 1893–1895). As he listened to his patients' responses to his technique, Freud came to realize that he was, indeed, touching them in very profound ways that facilitated their ability to know what they had not known they could know. In this way, the process of "free" associations was born, as the analytic environment itself was seen to "catch hold of" (Breuer and Freud, p. 110) elusive thoughts.

Winnicott (1965, 1971) brought into the literature the conceptualization of the good-enough "holding environment" as a prerequisite for healthy development. Increased attention to aspects of the early environment that provide the infant with a sense of "being held" within the object world helps us, by analogy, to imagine how specific facets of the analytic process might come to provide that kind of holding (see, for example, Stern, 1985; Beebe and Lachmann, 1988). From the couch or comfortable chair that provides a literal sense of being held within the room, to the quiet and exclusivity of the chamber itself, to aspects of the analyst's presence (such as the quality of gaze, tone, or empathic resonance), the primary prerequisite for the analytic endeavor would seem to be the initial establishment of a sense of being held within the analytic space. The trajectory of this process metaphorically parallels our early moments of life, in which the rhythms of attunement between caretaker and child provide the foundations for communication and mutual meaning-making. These types of metaphors help to pull us back from our conscious rational understandings of self and other, toward the "background music": the multiplicity of nonverbal meanings that contain and constrain our interactions.

The most salient exploration of touch in the psychoanalytic literature in recent years has centered around the "holding" metaphor. However, there are many other modes of nonphysical touch that affect both analyst and analysand. Many of our metaphors (such as gaze, mirroring, empathic attunement, and amodal perception) have derived from the literature focusing on infant-caretaker interactions. These metaphors have helped us better understand aspects of interactions that are experienced as contact (albeit in somewhat elusive ways), as we postulate and refine our conceptions of the underlying mechanisms. For example, "role responsiveness" (Sandler, 1976) and "projective identification" (Klein, 1946) are each ways of trying to discuss how affective experiences and meanings are transmitted between individuals without use of overtly physical or verbal-symbolic[1] channels.

In each of these terms, we find references to ourselves as physical beings making contact with self and other in nonphysical ways. For example, in projective identification, unconscious phantasy becomes the vehicle for modifying one's perception and thereby one's experience of the object (Grotstein, 2000a). The distorted perception is experienced affectively by the recipient as an assault to his or her habitual sense of self. The reaction to this distortion then feeds the perception of the other. As analysts, to the extent that we can accept the distortion and then find a way to speak to it without overwhelming the other, there is an opportunity for growth and understanding. To the extent that we reject the projection reactively, we tend to keep in place the projection of the alienated or unacceptable aspect of self.

This process may be seen, for example, in the case of the angry patient who invites our anger and denies his or her own. To the extent that we are able to be aware of and to tolerate our own anger, we are better able to speak to it in a way that promotes understanding. If we have a sense of the anger having been evoked precisely because the patient could not tolerate having it within him- or herself, we can speak to the dilemma of acknowledging anger in light of the meanings engendered by his or her experiences of the world. In essence, we must be able to be angry and survive in the face of it in order to be of use to our patients, who, in turn, must be able to touch us with their experience in order to have any assurance that our interpreta-

---

1. I am using the term "verbal" in the sense of "verbal-symbolic" functions, as opposed to more sensory qualities of voice.

tions might be meaningful (see, for example, Winnicott's [1971] explications of the "use of the object").

In this chapter, I explore some of the theoretical underpinnings in the analytic literature that appear to shed light on how we touch one another in these profound yet elusive fashions. We use metaphors of touch without having clearly delineated how this contact occurs. However, observational studies and analytic theory now converge to offer a better understanding of the non-verbal intercommunicative processes that I group together under the rubric of "nonphysical touch." Early interchanges between infant and caretaker are viewed as a model for examining how nonverbal understandings help to structure our understandings of how sensory and affective experiences become symbolized and communicated from one person to another. A clinical illustration is used to explore some of the meanings and uses of nonverbal modes of touch within the analytic environment.

THE DEVELOPMENT OF SYMBOLIC CAPACITY: THE IMPORTANCE OF ADEQUATE "HOLDING" OR "CONTAINMENT"

As we attempt to understand how meanings are interchanged without verbal or physical contact, we are led back to the early regulatory systems, which are primarily dyadic (Tronick et al., 1998). Interpersonal resonance continues to provide important information throughout the life cycle. In intimate dyads, such as those of mother/infant or analyst/patient, "the rhythms of behavior of the two partners are always coordinated, in some ways, usually out of awareness" (Beebe and Lachmann, 1998, p. 509). Reciprocal interactions often occur too quickly to be explainable by stimulus response models and may be more usefully described in terms of "coregulation" (Fogel, 1992), in which each partner's actions are continuously modified by the actions of the other. In this type of interaction, the partners do not match one another exactly, but rather each anticipates the movements of the other, in reciprocal patternings that tend to move in the same direction affectively. Stern (1985) described this process in terms of "matching the gradient," in which it is the configural aspects—such as intensity, timing, and form—that are being matched. Through this type of matching process, affective resonance becomes a palpable though subtle form of intercommunication, directing and modifying both thought and behavior.

In this way, affective resonance goes beyond distinct categorical states, to include all aspects of experience associated with those states. Stern's (1985) work has helped us to focus more explicitly on experiential qualities of affect that are primarily dynamic and kinetic, and pertain to the contour of experience—such as "fleeting," "decrescendo," or "explosive." These "activation contours" provide a useful rubric from which to explore interactive interpersonal experiences, such as affective attunement and interpersonal touch. My sense is that these contours have both evocative and symbolic functions, which come to represent experiences of being touched.

For example, as the mother holds the infant and soothes him or her with calming tones, the tone becomes overlain with the actual physical experience of being held in a soothing fashion. As the infant develops, the tone can serve the same function as had the physical experience of touch. In this way, the tone comes to "hold" the infant within the object world and also within him- or herself, and helps to provide a regulatory function. Over time, this regulatory function becomes integrated into aspects of self soothing, as when a child is observed to comfort herself via her doll, using the mother's soothing tone: "*It's* all right. Mama will be *right* back." Tone and prosody come to carry meaning beyond—and often in disjunction to—the words expressed. There are many times when patients do not hear our words at all, but only the tone, rhythm, or prosody, which conveys important elements of meaning, rather like the child who complains about being "yelled at" when there has been no increase in volume, but rather some note of disapproval in the tone.

Visual cues also carry meaning. For example, Stern (1985) noted the human propensity to attend to stimuli arrayed in the general configuration of the human face and form. Optimally, this configuration becomes associated with the onset of soothing regulatory functions. The gaze becomes a signal of presence, of soothing, of feeling "held." It can also represent an invitation to be known, or a prohibition against same. The ability to find one's self within the gaze of the other is an important facet of development (Winnicott, 1971), complemented by the mother's ability to see the child as a separate agent (Fairbairn, 1952; Fonagy and Target, 1997).

Just as the mother's receptivity is an important aspect of self-development, so, too, the analyst's receptivity is an integral part of the emergent organization facilitated by the patient/analyst relationship (Beebe and Lachmann, 1998). We know from the literature on disruption and repair in dyadic relationships that the child becomes acutely distressed in the face of an unresponsive mother (Tronick, 1989). This alerts the analyst to be aware of the implications of her own apparent nonresponsiveness. For individuals who have little expectation of engagement with an other, the visual affirmation of one's value as a unique and separate self may be a particularly important part of the analytic interchange (Hymer, 1986), a bedrock on which all later work can be built. Hymer (1986) suggested that "patients often require the affective engagement stimulated by eye contact with the analyst who is able to provide the gleam in the eye necessary for the development of trust and self-affirmation" (p. 156). For the patient who has experienced a parent as hostile or disengaged, it may be particularly important to be able to see the analyst's face in order to assure one's self that one is in the presence of a benign or benevolent, but separate, object (Hymer, 1986; Charles, 1999c).

THE SYMBOLIZATION OF EXPERIENCE: INTERTWINING VERBAL AND NONVERBAL DOMAINS

Development proceeds, at times precariously, between the poles of symmetry and separation, through which the self becomes defined within the context of sufficient sameness to provide an anchor in the external world, and sufficient differentiation to facilitate growth. This interplay is also found in the domain of meaning and symbol usage. As distinctions between self and other are refined, the emergent perspective facilitates the capacity for empathic awareness of the other. One need not *be* the object in order to be *with* the object. One may touch without merger; one may be soothed by the presence of the other without the necessity of physical contact. The imperfect character of the caregiver's reflective functions ensures that the child's introjection "will be of a *symbolic representation* rather than an *actuality*" (Target and Fonagy, 1996, p. 475).

This transition from symbolic equation to symbolic representation is an important one (Segal, 1957). Our ability to form and manipulate symbols allows us to better communicate subtleties of experience-as-lived. Sensory and affective experience can be particularly difficult to communicate in verbal form. However, we do seem to be quite adept at passing along information via matching processes of facial movements and vocal rhythms that eventuate in a recreation of the psychophysiological state of the other, thereby approximating the subjective state, as well (Beebe and Lachmann, 1998). In this way, nonverbal communications of sensory and affective experience often occur through interactive experiences of affective resonance, a form of nonphysical touch.

Bion (1965), picking up a theme alluded to by Klein (1963) in her later works,[2] noted the recursive nature of the connections between the paranoid-schizoid and depressive positions, by which the verbal informs the nonverbal and vice-versa, as ostensible realities become fragmented and reintegrated in accordance with new information. This would seem to represent the essence of growth and development, in which one's view of "reality" must be shaken in some way in order for a more complex view to intervene and become integrated. These two distinct modes of understanding—the paranoid-schizoid more experience near, the depressive more abstracted from experience—optimally interact

---

2. I am grateful to James Grotstein for bringing this to my attention.

to enlarge understanding. Affective awareness, in particular, becomes elaborated in the interplay between the concrete instantiation and the abstraction into categories of verbal understanding. In this way, "repeated observations of an object form functionally equivalent classes and prototypic images" (Bucci, 1997b, p. 195). These idiosyncratic generalized notions of reality then become what Bowlby (1973) and others have described as "working models" of self and other, based on the individual's ongoing history of affective interchanges.

Optimally, our sensory and affective awarenesses work in conjunction with our capacities for abstract, categorical thinking. However, the literature on infant observation and the work of theorists who have focused on the development of mentalization processes converge to suggest the importance of attending more pointedly to these more elusive sensory knowings within the analytic process. For some individuals, this may be a necessary precursor for establishing the safety of an analytic space. For others, it may be the primary mode of communication and understanding. In the clinical material to follow, I will explore how attention to the sensory and affective aspects of our interchanges can help us better understand diverse aspects of touch within the analytic process.

ATTENDING TO NONVERBAL COMMUNICATIONS

As we begin to pay more attention to nonphysical aspects of touch, we enhance the possibility of what have been described variously as "heightened affective moments" (Beebe and Lachmann, 1994) or "moments of meeting" (Stern et al., 1998). Bion described these moments of intense affective engagement as "passion," which he considered to be a fundamental element of the psychoanalytic process. "For senses to be active only one mind is necessary: passion is evidence that two minds are linked" (Bion, 1963, p. 13). These links offer an opportunity to see with both one's own eyes and those of the other: literally to re-vision realities that have become opaque and fixed. In order to discover the familiar in the unfamiliar, we have to be able to stand in some new relation to it. The very presumption of meaning can create openings by which previously unseen meanings might be received and elaborated.

When we tune our unconscious to that of the other, we are affirming the possibility that meaning might be transmitted in ways beyond rational interchange. As we become "lost" in the process, we also maintain an observing ego through which to make sense of our experiences, thereby affirming the essential importance of grounding our understandings in these primary moments of being and being-with. In this way, movements toward being-with may also be viewed as a fundamental return to the self as source, as the individual is afforded the opportunity to find his or her own rhythms that had receded to the background and become inaudible. Although there is often a regressive feel in moving toward these primary rhythms, there is also a great deal of potential: the "inherent rhythmic capacity of the psychophysical organism can become a source of order that is more stable than reliance on an order imposed either from outside, or by the planning conscious mind" (Milner, 1957, p. 224).

In moving closer toward our own sensory experiences and in affirming the interplay that takes place between self and other at these primary levels, we affirm the roots of our own creativity, derived from early experiences of self and other, self within other, and other within self (see chapter 5). This is a crucial vantage point for the analyst's reverie, which facilitates the transformation of sensory experience into elaborated meanings within the analytic hour. This reverie, during which the analyst's mind attempts to configure itself in accord with that of the patient, provides the kind of dyadic encounter that serves fundamental organizing and transforming functions (Sander, 1985; Tronick, 1989). To the extent that we can have faith in this transformative aspect of our silence, we facilitate the patient's ability to "find" him- or herself from within, rather than having it seemingly interposed from without. In this way, we provide a facilitating environment within which the patient can find his or her own creativity, rather than having it "stolen by a therapist who knows too much" (Winnicott, 1971, p. 57).

There is a crucial link between Milner's (1957) suggestion that a work of art only contains life to the extent that it bears the imprint of the person creating it, and Ogden's (1995) depiction of the crucial function of the analyst as bringing forth the possibility of greater aliveness. This link points to the primacy of the patient in the fundamental analytic task of bringing to life nuances of experience that had been lost due to a lack of appreciation of their inherent meanings and potentialities. This can be particularly important when working with individuals who feel unseen or unknown.

With Elena, for example (see chapter 5), the absolute prerequisite for any work to take place was some assurance that I could know her at a very profound level. This reassurance could not take place by words alone, but rather was sought in moment-by-moment scanning of my face for signs of recognition, acknowledgment: signs of psychic life. In fact, she had little use for my words at all, having so many, herself, with which to fill the hours. And yet, paradoxically, she also sought the very words she fended off. Her fears tended to preclude her ability to hear the words that might acknowledge her own reality and, in this way, might touch without annihilation.

At the bedrock of this work is the ability to be present with another being. This facility to work with the nonverbals—the relative intangibles of human interaction—is an important facet of the analyst's medium (as Milner [1957] used the term). Milner depicted the relationship between artist and medium as one of union, of knowing the other well enough to both know it as other and to also be completely present within it. This is the foundation upon which any analysis is built: the integrity of the relationship.

When we are able to create these conditions within the analytic space, we are able to touch one another in ways that profoundly alter our capacity to be and to be-with. This resonant attunement facilitates our ability to create symbols together through which the inner life might be better expressed, and through which we might see anew that which we had come to not-see, by force of habit or prohibition (Milner, 1957; Charles, 1998). This is done by

unmasking old symbols and making new ones, thus incidentally making it possible for us to see that the old symbol was a symbol; whereas before we had thought the
symbol was a "reality" because we had nothing to compare it with: in this sense. . . continually destroying
"nature" and re-creating nature [Milner, 1957, p. 229].

Within this process, what Bollas (1987) referred to as the
"unthought known" can be formally represented and thereby
more fully known. One example of this can be seen in my work
with David, for whom words tend to be diversions: shields against
invasion. As I probe into the meanings of his words, he is forced
to become conscious of their obstructive force that keeps him
safely but terribly alone. In this way, old meanings become open
to reconsideration: meaning itself becomes something that he
can contemplate sharing without annihilation.

In our struggles to give words to our inner life, the body is
often an articulate depicter and decipherer of metaphor. Our
willingness to sit with the language of the body (what Alvarez
[1997] referred to as the "grammar" of the body) facilitates the
relatively free interplay between levels of conscious and unconscious, and between verbal and nonverbal ways of knowing. Our
willingness to receive information from our bodies, and from
the nonverbal messages we receive from our patients, communicates to the patient that there is meaning to be found in these
primary experiences. This faith helps to ground the person in
his or her own corporeal realities and to encourage attention to
the subtleties and nuances of experience that might inform our
understandings.

The term "metaphor" comes from the Greek, meaning "to
transfer," implying a transference of meaning from one thing
to another. This transference is the essence of empathic attunement and intermodal responsiveness, as we communicate
essence without becoming quite so lost in the abstractions that
may mask the underlying meanings. Arlow (1979) suggested that
"metaphor can be understood in a more general way as a fundamental aspect of how human thought integrates experience
and organizes reality" (p. 368). The metaphoric relationship creates

a distance between the reality referred to and the mode of expression, which makes it easier to think about each, as well as the relationship between the two. In this way, it introduces the transitional space and facilitates the ability to play with ideas and meanings (Winnicott, 1953, 1971).

For individuals for whom the translating function between nonverbal and verbal domains of knowing has been inhibited—whether because the experiences were originally encoded via sensory channels alone, without verbal encoding, or whether trauma has inhibited the ability to know what one had known (or might have known if it had not been unknowable)—much of the communication within the treatment may be through sensory and affective channels. At these times, the individual's ability to touch us in ways that allow us to know what cannot be spoken interplays vitally with our own ability to utilize these same functions. In this way, our facility in the intermodal aspects of experience becomes a crucial factor in the treatment, undergirding the individual's capacity to become known and to also communicate that awareness in verbal form. In contrast, for those for whom the nonverbal track has become relatively mute, the task becomes one of moving beyond the words to the "sensory floor" of experience (Grotstein, 1985). The ostensibly unknowable has its own presence (Charles, 2001d). We struggle to navigate around these holes in experience, trying to find ways in which the unknowable can be tolerated sufficiently to touch some of its edges without fragmentation.

NONVERBAL COMMUNICATION AND THE PSYCHOANALYTIC PROCESS: ATTUNEMENT AND INTEGRATION

Although psychic growth has been postulated as the ultimate aim of analysis, this may be conceptualized quite differently. For many analysts, the goal would be one of becoming more alive or present in one's experience (see, for example, Bion, 1965; Ogden, 1995). Our own ability to "stay alive" within the moment facilitates the patient's ability to be present, as well. Winnicott (1971) discussed this in terms of "being" as opposed to merely existing. He saw being and becoming as active, life-enhancing, creative processes, full of meaning and vitality. Becoming, in this sense, often entails a continuing process of making manifest that which has remained as background, eluding our attention and verbal understanding. The process of "making the unthought thinkable" (Bianchedi, 1991, p. 11) involves a continual dialectic between the conscious and unconscious—or verbal and nonverbal—modes of being. To this end, the function of "the interpretation should be such that the transition from *knowing about* reality to *becoming real* is furthered" (Bion, 1965, p. 153). One important facet of this endeavor is to learn to attune ourselves with our patients sufficiently that we might touch, yet with enough distance that we might better elucidate meanings between us.

In our work, there is often a sensory experience of pattern, either affective or somatic, that becomes a cue or signal inviting our attention. Meanings may be conveyed through the prosody of the patient's speech, a countertransference reaction, or some other aspect of the process. For example, when a patient appears extremely distressed and we have no affective resonance to the distress, we are being provided with important cues that go beyond the visual or auditory. At these times, it is the lack of correspondence between the perceptual modalities that becomes the cue inviting our attention.

Rayner (1992) noted that the analytic enterprise is built on empathic attunement to preverbal events. It is through the emotional resonance, or matching, of the patient's rhythms or patterns that primary meanings become elucidated. This emotional resonance is a profound way of touching and being touched by the other. Often these experiences are cross-modal in nature and may be very difficult to articulate. The pattern may bear the form of an affective contour—or sensory melody—that carries its own meaning, if we can only be receptive enough to discover it (Stern, 1985). Attempts to articulate or communicate this function are often elusive, very similar to the difficulties encountered in describing other complex and subtle processes, such as projective identification. We may have a sense of being affected by the other through the subtle processes of mutual and self-regulation described by infant researchers (Beebe and Lachmann, 1994). At these times, articulating the meaning of our sensations may be less important than being receptive to their impact on each member of the dyad.

In chapter 3, I described how patterned movements become entries into the interactive meanings of self and other. I have wondered how my movements become informed by those of the other, as we communicate meanings through our bodies that our conscious minds cannot yet comprehend. At times, the reciprocal rhythms seem to have a soothing quality and I have wondered whether my self-soothing has become the other's own, facilitating tolerance or enshrouding essential terrors. In this way, nonphysical touch within the analytic space would seem to stem most directly from the affective field within the session. At times, this field may be so tangible that we feel enveloped or assaulted by it, potentiating what may be some of the most difficult and yet productive moments in the work: those moments of meeting when the experience of being-with is heightened and the possibility of change seems palpable.

CASE ILLUSTRATION

For many patients, my desire to touch and be touched by them is in keeping with their own desires to make contact within the interpersonal world. For others, however, the experience of being touched by another person is far more problematic, as is the case with the young woman I have referred to as "Nina" in chapter 3 (see also Charles, in press). After all this time, we are still in the process of negotiating her ability to enter into the space we are creating in my consulting room. There is always a disjunction for Nina in entering into my world. She comes to each session reluctantly, even when she has carried our relationship within her in a positive manner over the most recent interval. It may be at those very times that the disjunction is most severe, as her fantasy of being together becomes assaulted by the reality of my actual presence.

For some individuals, being-with has meant assault, intrusion, and even annihilation of self. For Nina, who describes an extremely narcissistic mother who insists on being the only frame of reference within the household, being-with has meant not-being or being other. Nina was never able to find a comfortable place for herself within the interpersonal world of her home, nor in the larger world, in which she felt tortured and tormented. She longed to "fit in," and finally managed to do so in college, but only at a huge price to her sense of self, which became even more split than before.

When I first met her, Nina was completing a second undergraduate degree program, but was thwarted by her inability to accommodate well enough to the dictates of the professional world to make a home for herself there. She still mourns this failure, which has been devastating for her. She now works at a job for which she is eminently overqualified, pouring her intelligence and creativity into reading and writing, and her yearnings for closeness into her relationships with animals.

When I first began working with Nina, she was like a startled doe: frozen, ready to run. Her smile is vivid but deceptive, often masking fears of being assaulted in some way she had not yet anticipated, but was struggling to ascertain. Over time, it became clear that Nina's main soothing devices have been music and mathematics: she will run a theme or pattern through her head in an attempt to allay her anxieties. At times, this ruse is relatively successful, whereas at other times a musical theme will intrude itself into her, becoming a further source of anxiety, agitation, and fear. Nina also attempts to manage her inner conflicts by writing about them in a novel in which the central character is based on a disowned version of self.

Nina has been perplexed by her intuitive senses, which in some ways help to keep her safe in a dangerous world, but also keep her vigilant and at the mercy of forces seemingly beyond her control. Nina's pattern for this view of reality was her mother, who brought in a seemingly endless succession of "new age" world views in her own attempts to explain the unexplainable, in her search for some meaning that would leave her at its core.

It was as though Nina's mother needed to forcibly lay these thoughts into her daughter's consciousness, but had no sense of Nina as a living, thinking human being who would be able to actually take them in and make sense of them.

Nina would become caught between her mother's insinuation that Nina could never truly understand whatever dogma was being elucidated, and her mother's assumption that of course Nina would accept whatever was accepted by the mother. In this way, being-with became the same as being-like in a symmetrization of self and other in which important distinctions could not be made (see Matte-Blanco, 1988) without a disruption in the parent-child bond.

Nina's mother appeared to have had little sense of her daughter as a separate person with her own mind and feelings. No one in her family had ever seemed interested in Nina's perspective or had asked her how she felt: "If I was upset about something when I was a kid, if I came home upset, I would tell my parents, and they would just never even say anything. I would go to my room and I would hear my dad say, 'Nina seems upset,' and my mother would say 'yes,' but no one would ever come talk to me or anything or show any interest."

My response to Nina came from my own resonance with her depiction: "It was as though you were a thing—like saying the television is broken, or the cable is out." At times such as these, my resonance soothes Nina and the work deepens.

I have needed to learn the meanings of tone, gaze, and rhythm with Nina, much as she has had to learn my own. At times, when our rhythms have become too discordant, the best that she can do is to leave a curt message on my machine saying that she is discontinuing treatment. This act alerts me to the fact that I have become irretrievably lost to her in any positive sense. At these times, my task is to find a way to touch her with my words or tone, with sufficient "holding" to enable her to walk once again through my door. This containment occurs largely through my allowing her reality to touch my own, without trying to annihilate it and therefore her.

During the course of her treatment with me, Nina began to make plans to marry, but was perplexed by her wish to not be with this person with whom she also wished to join herself with some permanency. She spoke of a sense of inherent bondedness, a sense that the two were "meant for one another," and yet she often preferred to be alone. This apparent disjunction disconcerted and frightened her, making her feel guilty and perplexed. Her perceptions of his desires became mandates, in much the same pattern as those of her mother. She tried to be with her fiancé at the appointed times, but became bored and restless and longed to be alone. She had no way of telling him that she would rather do something else, without violating some unconscious conception of what it means to "be in love with" and therefore "want to be with" another person. Exploring Nina's simultaneous desires to be-with and not be-with me in our sessions helped us better understand her ambivalence regarding the need/desire to be with anyone; the terror of engulfment aroused in her by even the idea of closeness; and the rage she feels as her interpersonal needs become palpable to her.

In our work, the trajectory of individual sessions has tended to be one of startle and disruption, as Nina has encountered my otherness in the moment. In chapter 3, I described the interactive rhythms through which we find one another within the hour, which appear to play out as auto-sensuous forms, rhythmically interplayed cross-modally between us. I tend to be aware of these patterns as sensory forms, elaborated in tactile ways, in the rubbing of my fingers against one another and the attuned rubbing of Nina's hands against one another, in reciprocal patternings. My metaphors are often visually derived, whereas Nina's primary sensory modality is auditory. She experiences these patterns primarily in terms of musical themes that run through her awareness and soothe her toward a greater ease in my presence. In this way, analyst and patient struggle to build a dyad from the often discordant rhythms, assumptions, and interpretations that arise between us. A new dimension has been added to this struggle in Nina's growing need to have me speak to my understandings of these rhythms, so that my awareness doesn't supersede her own.

"It is turtle season again," she told me recently. The children in her neighbourhood had begun massing, once again, to torture and maim the turtles in the pond nearby. Nina tried to stop them, but felt very ineffective in the face of the children's determination and the parents' lack of responsiveness. She spoke, with outrage, of a young child who had darted across the street in front of her car that morning, without even a glance at approaching vehicles, until he stood safely and defiantly on the other side. Nina had been enraged; it was not clear at whom. I wondered silently about this aspect of Nina: how she darts in front of me—desperately, defiantly, her armor seemingly suffocating her.

Nina then spoke of walking over by the pond and seeing some debris at the edge. She poked at it with a stick and discovered that it was the central portion of a much larger mass of snapping turtle that was lying largely submerged. She marveled at the hugeness of it and at its slow, arrogant exit from her proximity. Nina's own arrogance and hostility had been kept safely at bay in the form of the alter ego she was building in her most recent novel. Her fiancé's hatred of this character had kept Nina safely, but horribly, alone.

With the approach of her wedding date, Nina talked a great deal about feeling caught by other people's needs and intentions, and described feeling more and more awkward at having to confront the existence of another person. As she spoke of her irritation at having to be engaged in interactions with her fiancé and her concerns at marrying someone from whom she frequently would like to escape, I wondered aloud whether she felt that she needed to be the snapping turtle in order to make safe her own surrounds. I wondered, further, if part of her difficulty in negotiating territories with others had to do with her difficulty in being a frame of reference in her home of origin. I told her that I was reminded of her descriptions of having been in distress as a child: how her parents never inquired into the sources of her discomforts, but rather defined her in her absence, without any reference to her own feelings or perspective.

As Nina tried to mark out a territory for herself within the infinitely enigmatic domain of interpersonal relationships, she was so vigilant for signs of danger or intrusion that it was difficult for her to approach the other with sufficient presence to feel her own way through the encounter. There was little interplay between self and other in any mutually interactive pattern. This had become the fundamental task of our work: to develop, implicitly, rules of engagement in which neither self nor other would become lost.

What complicates this endeavor is Nina's sense of danger as an other approaches. To the extent that I can be in tune with her, I become soothing, but also dangerous. And so, the trajectories of our interactions tend to take the form of the startled and suspicious infant at reunion with the unreliable mother. As the mother slowly, over time, learns the intricacies of her child's rhythms, the child may, in reciprocal measure, allow herself to be soothed sufficiently to suffer another absence. To need the other is problematic, however, and so Nina attempts to not-need me, becoming enraged by her need of me, so that by the time she once again enters the interim space, she is caught between the desire for closeness and the armament of defenses she has built to protect herself from that very desire. The other danger inherent in this seduction is whether she will have to disown the hateful parts of herself in order to be loved. Will losing herself be the inevitable price of "acceptance"?

At a recent session, Nina arrived late and I had opened the door to my waiting room, to see if perhaps she had entered without my awareness. I could see her approaching the waiting room through the outer glass door and greeted her when she opened it. This disruption of her routine did not allow her the opportunity to sit down in the intervening space between the outer and inner worlds, as is her custom. She seemed to have even more difficulty than usual in encountering me, and to find it difficult to think of anything about which she might want to speak. The idea of speaking to me at all seemed problematic. Later, as she was talking about the difficulties she faces in encounters with others, and of the terrible intrusion she experiences when faced by the demands of an other's need or intent, I wondered whether her discomfort in this particular session had to do with my own intrusiveness at surprising her at the beginning of the session in that way and thereby disrupting our rhythms.

"Oh," she said, "I hadn't even thought of that. I do wonder sometimes whether you set things up like that on purpose." At such moments, I become dangerous, as Nina is assaulted by the unseen hands of some remote and uncaring, omniscient and omnipotent mother, who sets the stage according to her own inscrutable designs.

Nina is caught in a world in which touch becomes equated with intrusive assault, and in which being-with becomes engulfment. She becomes caught between my presence and my absence: both the corporeal disjunction and the affective one. She is exquisitely sensitive to these, and demands a quality of engagement, at times, that brings us into the heightened realm that Stern et al. (1998) described as "moments of meeting." As difficult as it may be for her to encounter my view of her in the moment, it would seem to be preferable to the uncertainty she experiences at feeling as though she is being seen from the other side of a lens into which she has not been invited to peer.

She prods me, much as she prodded the turtle, to see whether, indeed, I am merely more debris, or whether I might have some capacity for real engagement. She is not bothered by the turtle who protects himself, but only by the children who attack as though some very real being were merely refuse. I would imagine that she has been screaming inwardly at those children for a very long time. Her internal pleas for recognition have largely given way to hostile assaults in her conscious imagery, vivified now by the alter ego in her novel whom she describes as "waiting in the wings": the angry, violent child, who at times takes over her reverie and will not be stilled.

During this period, Nina brought in a dream that depicted vividly the terror she experiences in regard to other people:

She was outside the house of a childhood friend. It was an old mansion filled with interesting things and secret passageways. She was carrying two of her cats, but one jumped down and ran away. She tried to catch it, but it ran beyond the grounds and she couldn't follow it. She was concerned, but then became distracted by a car pulling up and reassured herself that the cats would turn up at the picnic later. Nina entered the house through the kitchen door and moved toward the stairway to the second floor. As she neared the stairs, the cellar door opened. The opening was black and gaping, and she was very frightened. As she started to go upstairs, there was a force, like a vacuum, pulling her back toward the cellar. She was terrified, but managed to get herself up the stairs, into a room, and then to shut the door. She lay down on a bed and became aware that she was actually sleeping and could rouse herself if she tried. However, she was unable to awaken. She then decided that if she let herself fall deeper into sleep, she would be able to wake herself up. She tried out this plan several times. Each time she tried to awaken herself, she would open one eye and see details of her actual room, but then the rest of the room would be just as it was in the dream and she would know that she had not managed to get out of it.

Finally, there was a knock at the door. Nina's terror increased as the door opened, and then abated as she saw her fiancé standing there. She told him that she needed to get out of there and they went downstairs together, coming upon her mother and grandmother, who were standing in the open doorway. Her mother was wearing a flowered dress, "as though it was summer and they had just wandered in." As they stood there, Nina felt an urge to punch her mother. She said that she knew it was a dream, so she did punch her and it felt good and her mother didn't respond, so she kept punching, with increasing energy. She was enjoying this a great deal, and then realized she could kick, too. As she was punching and kicking, her boyfriend and grandmother rather weakly told her to stop, but she ignored them. Finally, she pushed her mother out the door and onto the ground, and then ran off.

This dream illuminated how frightened Nina becomes, how she closes herself off from the world, and how all of her failures have become persecutors that keep her locked inside of herself. Contact in the dream is precarious and unreliable, and the pain of it is denied.

Notable in this dream, however, was the possibility of facing one's fears. This new potentiality was in striking contrast to the air in an earlier dream, in which Nina had been trying to find a passage through a cellar and had been confronted by a towering, terrifying woman who seemed to walk right through her. Nina lost consciousness in the dream, falling to the ground in a flurry of flower petals.

I said that I wondered if part of what she was doing in the current dream was telling herself that she didn't have to be so frightened of some of the things that scared her; that she had internal resources she could bring to bear. She made a comment regarding my putting a positive spin on things (which of course I was), but then let me continue. I said that I was thinking that when we have been humiliated in the past, we may avoid looking at people, because they seem very powerful and even evil, and then we don't have the opportunity to see that they are just lost and not so terribly powerful. I said that it reminded me of the woman at Nina's workplace whom she had viewed as evil, whom she had described as her nemesis, until one day when the woman had felt left out of a conversation and revealed her own vulnerability. Nina said, "Yes, but then I saw the pain, and that was just as bad, because it was so terrible to see."

In that moment, I realized how caught she was between trying to keep the other at bay by keeping them evil and dangerous, versus being engulfed by the terrible poignancy of the pain of the other, which threatens to suck her down into the void, like the blackness of the cellar in the dream. That would seem to parallel the dilemma in which she has been caught with her mother (and grandmother) all these years. She has desperately needed her mother to be real: to stop playing in her fantasy world of psychic "powers" and to make contact with the reality of her daughter's pain. However, when Nina has insisted on obtaining her mother's attention, she has been called to task by her father for "hurting" her mother in so cold-hearted a fashion. This dilemma has been most notable as she has begun to grapple with her relatively recent awareness of having been abused by her grandmother, a reality her mother insists on keeping at bay. Her family, characteristically, has been unwilling to know the unknowable and has ostracized the Nina who knows.

Nina was terribly distressed and was crying quite heavily when we reached the end of this session. I let her sit for a few minutes and then, with a great deal of hostility, she asked, "Why aren't you telling me to leave?" She left with a lot of heat: I imagine that her anger helped her to go. It was probably important for her to be able to be the angry child with me, to run past defiantly as I approached her, and to attack me for moving closer even as we approached this imminent and seemingly ultimate end. She continues to attack me, much as she attacks her fiancé, needing to bristle against the discomforting closeness and to know whether she can be all sharp edges and still be held safely.

Nina's tremendous sensitivity is both a blessing and a curse, a legacy of her need to be vigilant in the face of insufficient maternal attunement. It informs the characterizations and landscapes of her novels and dreams, and allows her to appreciate many of the joys of life with a finely tuned ear or eye. However, it has made her interpersonal world a nightmare, which she longs to decode or escape from, and has also impeded her ability to use her own sensory and affective experiences in the service of meaning making. Nina's hostility is a palpable force in the room and I encounter it to some degree at each meeting. At times she is like a porcupine, bristling at signs of imminent danger; at times she is like a wounded animal in pain, longing for surcease, yet likely to attack if approached.

I spend these moments with Nina trying to attune myself sufficiently to her key that my voice might touch without biting, that my glance might touch without intrusion, that I might be with her in a manner that facilitates her being with herself sufficiently to engage, in some measure, in the type of joint effort that seems to call to her mockingly, and yet continually eludes and evades her. Although there are more moments of meeting these days, there are also times when there is little that is soothing about our moments of touching, except for that which resides in the awareness that there may not be a precipice waiting; in the possibility that all parts of self might be held without falling into the abyss; or perhaps merely in the idea that we might not have to wander these regions alone.

CONCLUSION

The nonverbal aspects of experience are in some ways subtle and easily overlooked. However, they are also powerful forces that impinge upon our awareness continually. In the analytic space, being with the other entails a willingness to be with parts of self that have been disowned or remain unintegrated. These aspects of self are experienced as sensations that pass back and forth between analyst and analysand in what are often highly ambivalent attempts to metabolize them. Our ambivalence often takes the form of a game of "hot potato," giving rise to terms such as "projective identification" and "role-responsiveness," as each partner to some extent disowns facets of whatever might be known between the two. Our willingness to be touched by the experience of the other provides an opportunity to translate the patterns we discover into mutually created meanings that can be held by each, without annihilation.

5

FOUNDATIONS OF CREATIVE EXPRESSION: PRIMARY EXPERIENCE AS CREATIVE POTENTIAL

*W*hen I first encountered Elisabeth Vigée-Lebrun's portraits, I was struck by the difference in feeling tone between her own self-portraits and those she had painted of other mothers with their children. In these works, I sensed that a statement was being made about the importance of connectedness between parent and child. Depictions of mother and child offer a unique vantage point from which to make conjectures regarding links between modes of representation and the individual's history and vision of self and world. As a result, it was interesting to find in the memoirs of Vigée-Lebrun (1903) explicit statements as to the importance of her early life with her parents for her own sense of well-being, as well as critical observations about mothers who put other cares before their children. An astute but very forgiving judge of people, Vigée-Lebrun's vision has a clearly positive aura that pervades her works (see Figure 5.1).

As we try to understand the creative process—how it develops and how it flourishes—there seem to be two opposing pathways, each of which begins in the earliest experiences between self and other. Analysts tend to be most familiar with a view of creativity as originating in the storm and stress of difficult relationships with self and universe. However, there would seem to

103

Figure 5.1. Elisabeth Vigée-Lebrun, *Portrait of the Artist With Her Daughter,* 1789. Musée du Louvre. Copyright Réunion des Musées Nationaux/Art Resource, NY.

be an equally important line that flows from the type of nurturing and supportive environment that allows the talents of the budding artist to flower relatively free from strife. Whichever line we are attending to, as we focus on the early moments of life, we can see that self and world become defined within the context of relationships and cannot be understood without an appreciation of the patternings that evolve from early object relations. Early experiences become the ground on which the world is structured. They manifest themselves in patterns that play and replay over the course of a lifetime. These experiences may be far greater determinants of the forms that are created than of the existence of creativity per se (see Machotka, 1992).

We may never truly know the origins of creativity itself, and yet we may be enriched by trying to trace factors that influence how creativity becomes manifest. Any real understanding of these factors will require some attention to how nonverbal meanings are transmitted, an essential aspect of any creative process. Nonverbal communications are an innate and fundamental way of exchanging information about feelings and interests (Trevarthen, 1995). They tend to recede further to the background with the development of language and yet are registered and utilized, whether or not we are overtly conscious of them (see McLaughlin, 1993; Jacobs, 1994). As Rhode (1998) put it: "Feelings require forms to articulate themselves" (p. 257).

THE PARENT/CHILD RELATIONSHIP AS ORGANIZING PRINCIPLE

As we look at various artists' depictions of mother and child or of self in relation to world, we can notice many subtleties that give us clues as to how relationships are patterned for that particular individual. We can note, in the relative proximity of the figures and in the relative tension of their bodies, some of the artist's notions of what it means to be-with and to not be-with another and with one's self. One striking portrayer of this theme is Ana Mendieta (1948–1985), a Cuban performance artist who was exiled from her home and parents in early adolescence.

What are left of many of her performances are photographs of Mendieta's body encased in earth or, alternatively, the imprint left by her body in the ground (see Figure 5.2). In repetitive enactments in which her body created a space for itself within the earth or, alternatively, became covered with earth, Mendieta's art depicts strikingly her longings for reunion with mother and with mother earth.

As Mendieta, herself, put it:

I have been carrying out a dialogue between the landscape and the female body (based on my own silhouette). I believe this has been a direct result of my having been torn from my homeland (Cuba) during my adolescence. I am overwhelmed by the feeling of having been cast from the womb (nature). My art is the way I re-establish the bonds that unite me to the universe. It is a return to the maternal source. Through my earth/body sculptures I become one with the earth. . . . I become an extension of nature and nature becomes an extension of my body. This obsessive act of reasserting my ties with the earth is really the reactivation of primeval beliefs. . . . An omnipresent female force, the after-image of being encompassed within the womb, is a manifestation of my thirst for being [in Maure, 1996, p. 51].

Our experiences of feeling "held" in the world emerge from the early ability to evoke resonance from the parent. This holding (Winnicott, 1971) or containment (Bion, 1962, 1963) helps to develop the child's internal processing of attention, curiosity, and affective appraisal, which are so fundamental to "making sense" of self and others (Trevarthen, 1995). Children who do not sufficiently develop their own capacities for self-soothing and self-containment (Schore, 1994) may be missing what Tustin (1986) has referred to as the "rhythm of safety." These rhythms are often sought through the creative endeavor or, alternatively, the need for them may be denied.

This type of denial can result in art that is experienced as assaultive or jarring in some way, such as we might find in the

Figure 5.2. Ana Mendieta, *Serie árbol de la vida* (Tree of Life Series), 1977. Color photograph of earth/body work. Iowa: 20 × 13¹⁄₄ inches. Galerie Lelong, New York. Courtesy of the Estate of Ana Mendieta and Galerie Lelong, New York.

harsh brush strokes of certain painters whose early life was disrupted by death and tragedy. These would include, for example, Edvard Munch, who witnessed his mother's sudden death at the age of five and whose early life was colored by illness and tragedy (Steinberg and Weiss, 1954). We might think also of Egon Schiele, the Austrian painter working at the turn of the century, whose early relationship with his mother seems to have been disrupted as a result of his mother's grief over the death of his older sister, as well as complications associated with the birth of a younger sister, against a wider backdrop of illness and tragedy within the family (Knafo, 1993). The absence of mother requires, to some extent, the need to give birth to the self, as Schiele depicts in his *Dead Mother* portraits, the second of which he subtitles *The Birth of Genius* (see Figure 5.3). However, in the presence of hostile envy on the part of the mother, the creative urge itself may become paralyzed by fears of annihilation (Charles, 2001b), as in the case presented later in this chapter.

Art can provide a means for denying trauma and also for working it through. These attempts may be quite disparate, depending on the predominant defenses, which may range from the rigid and inhibiting, to excess (Machotka, 1992). Regardless of the particular type of defenses employed, art offers an opportunity to witness whatever could not be known by bringing into focus facets of our experience that have eluded our conscious awareness. Whether or not we can accept the challenge thus offered, the place has been marked. In this way, the objectified image provides an opportunity to re-work the type of profound absence that Loeb and Podell (1995) suggested is at the core of psychic trauma. Art offers an illusion of connectedness, an opportunity to experience "a state of emotional accord with a responsive presence" (Rose, 1996, p. 108). In that moment, one is not alone. Rose put it this way: "Art offers the wherewithal to create a preconscious illusion of a responsive presence—it offers an objective image of the experience of human feelings" (in Loeb and Podell, 1995, p. 992). Paradoxically, it can be our very aloneness that allows this feeling of connectedness.

Because creative acts often derive from sources that are not consciously known, profound subtleties of experience may be

Figure 5.3. Egon Schiele, *Dead Mother I*, 1910. Oil and pencil on wood, 12³/4 × 25.8 cm. Leopold Museum—Privatstiftung, Vienna.

portrayed explicitly in symbolic form. For example, Giorgio de Chirico's paintings vivify the intense isolation of his early life (Krystal, 1966). Notable in these paintings is an absence of real people. Human figures are most often depicted as statues, shadows, or faceless creatures. They are hardly discernible as human beings and tend to be placed in contiguity to one another without touching, even with the gaze (see Figure 5.4). In these paintings, the absent parent comes to configure a sense of the self as empty, so that a primary affective reaction to de Chirico's work is a sense of emptiness, desolation, and despair (Krystal, 1966).

As can be seen in the life and art of de Chirico, whose early experiences with a physically absent father and an emotionally distant mother presaged a lifetime of isolation and despair, the early interactions between parent and child have long-term consequences. These primary relationships affect our ability to take in and organize our experiences at very basic levels, including the structuring of our neuroanatomy in the early years of life (Trevarthen, 1989; Schore, 1994). Normal development, especially the ability to self-regulate affect, seems to depend on a "good-enough" experience with early caretakers. Deficits in this area constrain our capacity to take in sensory information and to form impressions regarding the patternings of this data, the foundation for all later learning. What cannot be taken in consciously is still taken in, stored as sense impressions or what Bion (1977) described as α and β elements. As these elements become patterned, they form our dream thoughts: primary sources of metaphor and imagery (Bion, 1977).

NONVERBAL WAYS OF KNOWING: CROSS-MODAL COMMUNICATIONS

Art is essentially an embodied experience: our perceptions are inevitably constrained by our encounters with form and substance (Merleau-Ponty, 1962, 1993). Consciousness arises in the context of the integrated operation of the senses (Crowther, 1993) and therefore cannot be truly understood without some acknowledgment of the body that structures and underlies all

Figure 5.4.   Giorgio de Chirico, *Portrait of the Artist With His Mother,*
1919. Oil on canvas. 31 × 21½ inches. Copyright
Christie's Images, London.

knowledge. Many of our understandings contain references to
our modes of perception. For example, the phrases "I see . . . ";
"I feel . . . "; "It seems . . . " each represents an attempt to frame
one's understandings in terms of the perceptual bases that
underlie them.

As development proceeds, sensory experience becomes patterned and organized. In this way, the dimensions of experience,
such as shape, texture, and location in space, all come to carry
meanings beyond any specific representation. We learn to "read"
nuances of line in works of art as in faces. The slope, the turn,
the sweep, the rhythm: each in some important way seems to
mirror the type of affective prosody described by such disparate
theorists as Stern (1985) and Tomkins (1962, 1987). Although
we may not be able to decode them in verbal terms, these types
of meanings become reference points utilized in dreams and
other creative endeavors (Charles, in press).

Development progresses, in part, through patterned experiences of rhythmicity that become the background "melodies" that inform our understandings of self, other, and world. These rhythms are grounded in the ongoing dyadic communications that facilitate the infant's growing capacity for self- and mutual regulation (Beebe, Lachmann, and Jaffe, 1997; Beebe and Lachmann, 1998). As knowledge is mirrored from one to the other, what is being learned is not only the overt communication, but also, more important, the very processes by which meanings become communicated.

These communications are cross-modal in nature (Stern, 1985). Our ability to translate meanings from one modality into another is an important aspect of the creative process, as meanings are digested and transformed (or expelled) through the medium of choice. Primary "knowings" or sensations become transliterated into affective intonations or rhythms that may pattern hue, tone, amplitude, and other dimensions of experience in ways that become communicated to the audience. Gauguin, for example, often talked about his painting in terms of "repetitions of tone" and other musical metaphors, referring to color as "vibration as well as music, attaining . . . nature['s] . . . interior force" (letter to Fontainas, March 1899; quoted in Rose, 1996, p. 55). This facet of painting would seem to call on the strengths of the more nonverbal, "intuitive" parts of the brain in which patterned events, such as prosody, are "read" (Trevarthen, 1995).

"Art communicates powerfully because it makes systematic expression of deep and spontaneous 'images' or 'impulses,' that are subjective, emotional, and therefore, immediately transferable" (Trevarthen, 1995, p. 160). Its power resides in being at once of the individual and of the community: it partakes of the universal through the particular. Part of what moves us in art derives from the feeling of the artist in the act of creation. The emotion is carried in the brush stroke or flourish: our ability to receive and convey information cross-modally enables us to ingest and integrate these disparate aspects of experience into fleeting impressions or enduring certainties that may or may not be consciously "known."

Memories become organized in terms of their affective tone and prosody, which convey essential information as to the scripting of that type of experience. This structuring leads to the development of generalized episodes: prototypical expectations against which later occurrences are gauged and modified (Stern, 1985). The patterns then become meaningful structures that can be modified, further elaborated, or encapsulated, depending on the individual's later experiences and how, and whether, they can be integrated. With an encapsulated experience, for example, you might see, as with the self-portraits of Frida Kahlo, a repetitive theme that becomes enacted over and over again without substantive change or development (Knafo, 1991). In contrast, one might look at the self-portraits of Egon Schiele, which do change over time, reflecting his developing sense of self (Knafo, 1993); or at Mondrian's series of trees, in which one can see increasing modifications and elaborations of a theme, resulting in a transformation of the works as they progress from the more concretely representational to higher and higher levels of abstraction. As the background becomes foreground, the essence of the form comes to take precedence over the content.

These generalized episodes appear to be linked by patterns— in linguistic terms "structural invariants" (Cooper and Aslin, 1994, p. 1676) or in Bion's terms "constant conjunctions"[1] (1965, p. 14)—that enable us to discriminate and respond to the relevant signals. Kris (1952) noted that art communicates to the audience through processes of recognition and kinesthetic reactions that give rise to experiences of participation or co-creation. These processes are facilitated by our ability to recognize cross-modal equivalencies and to transpose essential elements of meaning from one experience to another across domains (Stern, 1985). In this way, we may respond to a familiar pattern without consciously recognizing it. Often, it is the affective contour or rhythm of the experience that facilitates this understanding.

---

1. Constantly conjoined elements are those that are always found together and therefore seem to be linked in some fundamental way that may or may not be understood.

Experiences of affective attunement—or resonance with a responsive other—form the basis of amodal experiences, as the infant's experience is recast into some other form of expression (Stern, 1985). Rooted in this type of interactive sensory activity are both rhythmicity and the capacity to play (Rayner, 1992), essential underpinnings of creative activity.

The infant's experience is more primary than that of the adult, not yet translated into verbal categories that may override and obscure the basic patternings of experience as lived in the moment (Stern, 1985). The emergent organization of the subjective world inheres in the idiosyncratic patternings of experience, which are then projected onto the outer world. To the extent that the child is engaged in responsive interactions with significant others, a shared system of meanings evolves. To the extent that the child is isolated from the shared emergence of meaning, the patternings will be idiosyncratic. The creative act would seem to be born in the interstices between consensual and idiosyncratic meanings.

PATTERNED EXPERIENCE

Although fundamental patterns of experience may be more or less idiosyncratic, they can also be traced to culture and family and provide important information as to how an individual's world is ordered. Langer (1951) alluded to these patterns in her book *Feelings and Form,* in which she spoke of art as an abstraction that must always remain "true in design to the structure of experience. That is why art seems essentially organic; for all vital tension patterns are organic patterns" (p. 373). The abstraction helps to affirm the order, leaving it less obscured by the content, so that, for example, in the world of music: "tones hold up for our perception, as real, a dimension of the world that transcends all individual distinctions of things and therefore all verbal language" (Zuckerandl, 1956, p. 372).

These organic patterns have their roots in our earliest experiences and antedate the more explicit organization of conscious memory. The categories and expectations we build up, based on these patterned experiences, become the nonverbal foundations of symbolic thought. Nonverbal meanings are particularly important in affective interchanges and thus have a unique importance in the world of art, where a given product may be technically good, but its *greatness* often depends on the relative success in eliciting an affective response from the audience.

In this way, aspects of sensory experience—such as tone, gesture, touch, and facial affect—become prototypes or patterns that inform all later interactions. Memories of these experiences may be outside of explicit awareness and yet they become an important part of the unrepressed unconscious, sometimes termed "implicit memory," "procedural knowledge" (Clyman, 1991; Fonagy, 1998), or "implicit relational knowing" (Stern et al., 1998). All of these terms refer to a perceptual representational system that interacts with, but can also function independently of, semantic memory (Schacter, 1992).

Implicit memory seems to function largely through the perception and repetition of patterned experience, and functions more efficiently when we are not explicitly trying to remember. Examples include driving a car or playing a musical instrument: as our actions become routinized, we may perform better when we are not explicitly paying attention. Cézanne addressed this issue in reference to his painting. Although he was very interested in the more theoretical aspects of painting, he found that concentrating on his ideas interfered with his ability to do the work. "If I interpret too much," he said, "if today a theory carries me away which contradicts one of yesterday, if I think about it while painting, if I intervene, I get all fouled up" (in Podro, 1990, p. 402). In this way, too direct a focus can impede the ability to "play" with ideas: an important source of creativity (Winnicott, 1971).

The various forms of creative expression offer a means of replaying important patterns in new ways and thereby communicating to others (and to self) about meanings that may be beyond our conscious awareness. For example, Doris Lessing (1971) noted that one fantasy the writer has of the critic is that he or she will understand the work well enough to interpret back to the author whatever he or she had been missing. For many artists, the creative endeavor is both an assertion of self and an act of self discovery. There is an interplay with the audience, real or imagined, in which meanings become considered, elucidated, and transformed.

To some extent, we are always seeking our selves. Art is a way of putting forward aspects of self, that they might be considered from various perspectives and we might come to better "know" the self. The capacity to know one's own experience at a deep and fundamental level is an important aspect of creativity, constrained by the quality of the early attachment bonds (Fonagy and Target, 1997). There seems to be an optimal balance between responsiveness and disjunction; resilience seems to be facilitated by repeated sequences of disruption and repair within a normative range (Beebe and Lachmann, 1994). Too much responsiveness sets us up for an inevitable fall; too little creates the fall.

In either case, inadequate parenting tends to result in a perseveration, in which the individual repeatedly plays out patterns as a way of elucidating them or perhaps, at times, of obscuring the essential vulnerability underlying them. For the artist, this repetition can become a driving passion. We can see this tendency in the work of many artists, in terms of visual or literary themes that play out over and over, with only a change of character or locale. Think, for example, of the writer mentioned briefly in chapter 3, who replayed the same important themes and interpersonal relationships that had been salient and problematic in his childhood in the various plots and characters in both his dreams and novels. In this way, he expelled the problematic material, but also offered a means for exploring it.

The depiction of pattern becomes a way of making known to one's self whatever is important and yet remains unknown to the conscious mind. It also provides a means for reworking difficult truths and perhaps coming to terms with them. One may wonder, for example, to what extent Mary Cassatt's repetitive theme of "mother and child" in her paintings is a working through of her own feelings about remaining childless (see

Zerbe, 1987). Edvard Munch is more explicit in this regard, in speaking about having repeated the theme of the "sick child" so many times: "no other influence was possible than that which wells forth from my home. These pictures were my childhood and my home" (in Eggum, 1978, p. 146).

We can find another example of this type of perseveration in the films of Jean Cocteau, in which he plays out the theme of finding and losing and finding himself, over and over again. In his variations on the theme of "Orpheus," Cocteau focuses on aspects of the self as objects that can be considered and reconsidered, in an attempt to move beyond the ostensibly known toward what might become known from another perspective. For example, in the film *Blood of the Poet*, the protagonist draws a face. The mouth seems to come to life and the artist, startled, erases it when he thinks someone might be coming. In the act of erasing the mouth, it adheres to his own hand; whatever he had been trying to say or not say in depicting this mouth takes on a life of its own, as the mouth continues the quest for expression. This associational trail is the language of the unconscious, in which like becomes same and important distinctions between similar objects are lost (Matte-Blanco, 1975).

This type of symmetrization invites us into a symbiotic relationship with the artist: as we begin to appreciate the product, we are drawn into the very dilemma in which the artist is pinned. This absorption may take the form of participating in the nightmare of another, which also invites us into an investigation of that nightmare and thereby into possible resolutions. Through these richly condensed images we are invited to "discover the new and rediscover the familiar" (Oremland, 1997, p. 24), thereby discovering and rediscovering aspects of self and other. There is an ongoing dialectic between the meanings found in the similarities—or equivalencies—detected among disparate objects and those found via our more verbal/rational capacity to categorize by making distinctions between ostensibly similar things. It is in the interplay between these two types of meanings that art moves beyond the purely appealing and approaches transcendence.

Many experiences seem familiar because of the affective charge or prosody (melody) that may let us know that we are encountering something familiar in the guise of an ostensibly novel situation. This may be seen in the process of transference, in which we find ourselves behaving as though in the presence of "mother" when confronted with particular characteristics that have become associated with her. This tendency to symmetrize—to collapse distinctions between similar objects in the presence of strong emotion—is an important aspect of creative work. It helps us to jump across equivalencies to amplify meanings, as for example, in poetry, where one word may come to carry multiple associations that are affectively charged and therefore tend to engender a particular response that hits affectively before it begins to ripple semantically (see chapter 6). This is the power of metaphor (see, for example, Ingram, 1996).

The metaphoric relationship creates a distance between the "reality" referred to and the mode of expression. This is the continuing dialectic between processes of fragmentation and integration, as the essential elements are broken apart and then reconfigured in ways that call attention to possible meanings. As we puzzle over our experience and recreate it through various mediums, we provide an opportunity for both self and other to see in ways that are new or fresh. Edvard Munch stated this intention quite explicitly: "In my art, I have tried to explain to myself, life and its meaning. I have also intended to help others to more clearly understand life" (in Stang, 1972, p. 154).

For many artists, this process is less intentional and yet it still occurs. Our essential equilibrium depends on our ability to take in sensory data and to order it in a coherent fashion—to "make sense" of it. Intense, unmoderated emotions impede our ability to make important distinctions that help to order, organize, and give meaning to the world. Meaning may also be more actively denied through the destruction of meaningful links between self and other, and between cause and effect (Bion, 1967). Communication can be an invitation or may be used defensively, as a way of keeping others at bay. In either case, the nonverbal aspects of communication often provide important information as to how an individual's internal and external worlds are ordered. Even when the medium is ostensibly that of language, as in poetry, it is often the nonverbal aspects of experience that are being depicted through the medium of words.

ATTENDING TO NONVERBAL COMMUNICATIONS

In encountering a piece of art, there is a matching process, as we "tune" our unconscious to that of the other. These types of experiences are often cross-modal in nature and difficult to articulate, and yet our affective and sensory responses to a work affirm that meanings can be transmitted in ways beyond rational interchange. As we respond to the symbols being communicated through the artist's expressive attempts, meanings become elucidated. The symbols may be overt, as in the forms depicted and their relationships to one another, or they may be more covert. For example, many aspects of the process itself may be communicated through technical aspects of a work, such as intensity of hue, textural qualities, and other stylistic variations.

As we try to understand how the unknown becomes manifest in creative forms, Bion's (1962, 1963) work is of particular interest, in that it points to some of the essential paradoxes that confront us as we try to understand the evolution and communication of patterned forms in art. Bion's formulations were highly abstract and yet he profoundly appreciated the importance of being grounded in one's own experience. His views of thinking begin with relationships: between person and environment, or thinker and thought, each of which he refers to in terms of the "container" and "contained."

For Bion, there is no way of understanding one without the other: the container defines whatever is contained as surely as the contained defines and proscribes the container. This is, fundamentally, how learning works: meanings coalesce under the rubric of a given term, concept, or word and then, as our understanding of that concept changes, we devise new words to better "contain" the meaning. We run into difficulties with complex terms, such as "countertransference," whose meanings change over time without necessarily being sufficiently defined (contained) to facilitate the type of real communication that can further refine (contain) the concept and thereby enhance learning.

We also run into difficulties with feelings, which are difficult to define. A work of art can become a way of defining/containing nonverbal messages so that they can be communicated. The observer then becomes the container for the message, also transforming it in some way that either integrates and enriches the meaning(s), or constrains and rejects them. This process of metabolizing nonverbal information requires a medium through which the message might be contained in some way. The message itself then becomes a container of sorts in that it defines and proscribes whatever meanings inhere. Although this mode of conceptualization may seem convoluted, it is worth spending some time digesting, as it provides an important rubric for understanding the essence of creative processes. The concept is of particular relevance to the artist, who both uses and is used by the medium. One cannot really consider either without the other: each potentially transforms the other.

In line with current infant research, Bion (1963) suggested that the mother eases the child's encounters with the infinite by transforming and translating the primary experience into tolerable and meaningful chunks. As the mother contains the chaos, the "chunks" are contained and also become containers of meanings that can then be further elaborated and integrated. As development proceeds, we ease our own encounters with the infinite by transforming it in various ways (including artistic creations) through the use of symbols. Symbols allow us to play with aspects of experience that are not accessible to conscious thought, including whatever might be too terrifying if it were to be perceived as too "real."

In analytic work, we encounter many things that cannot be thought about, in spite of the need to understand them. Some of these experiences occurred before language had developed sufficiently to encode memories in that kind of way, whereas other experiences may not conform to our habits of thought. Often, what is unknown is so integral to our view of reality that we tend to overlook it. This is particularly true of ongoing experiences that become habitual. The creative act, whether in art or in analysis, provides a means for defamiliarization (Miall and Kuiken, 1994): for enabling us to look anew at what had become invisible (Symington, 1983; Parsons, 1988). The anomaly inherent in metaphoric representation provides an opportunity to re-vision:

> The purpose of art is to impart the sensation of things as they are perceived, not as they are known. The technique of art is to make objects "unfamiliar," to make forms difficult, to increase the difficulty and length of perception because the process of perception is an aesthetic end in itself and must be prolonged [Shklovsky, 1917, p. 12].

This type of foregrounding process fragments the ostensible reality, thereby inviting reinterpretation and reintegration of aspects of experience that had become occluded due to familiarization (Miall and Kuiken, 1994). In Bion's (1977) terms, foregrounding shapes a new "selected fact" that restructures our perceptions. In this way, it becomes the new containing context, prescribing how meanings should be construed.

The containing and metabolizing functions of the mother/child relationship (Bion, 1963) provide a useful rubric for understanding how primary experiences come to have idiosyncratic meanings. The mother contains the child's experiences by moderating them, by not allowing the child to become overwhelmed by too much stimulation. In this way, she also patterns the experience into categories and names them. These categories become linked with symbolic meanings, which can then be brought together to form more complex thoughts. The reversal of this process is the *unlinking* of associations, the denial of meaning (Bion, 1962). Acceptance, denial, and previous experience each patterns our conscious and unconscious understandings within the reciprocal exchange and elaboration of meanings.

There are many primary experiences that are unconscious, not due to repression, but by virtue of their structure, which cannot become conscious without being transformed in some fashion. The act of creating forms represents, to some extent, our experience of the lived moment, thereby containing some essential aspects of it, whether or not these are consciously known. From this perspective, art is one way of making primary experience more accessible by ordering the sensory experiences in ways that illuminate meanings, in the sense of *knowing* rather than *knowing about.* This process has been referred to as a "transformation" (Bion, 1965), or "translating" or "unfolding" function (Matte-Blanco, 1975), also described by Fonagy and Target (1997) as "mentalization" processes. For Cézanne, this type of transformative process was essential to creative work. He described painting as a process of allowing truths to emerge by keeping one's intellect from getting in the way, saying: "The landscape is reflected, is humanised, is thought in me. I objectify it, fix it on my canvas" (in Podro, 1990, p. 403). In this way, he refers to the artistic process as an interactive activity whereby both painter and subject are transformed.

SELF-EXPERIENCE AND THE CREATIVE PROCESS

The internal drive to create meaning wells, according to Milner (1952), from an "internal necessity for inner organization, pattern, coherence, the basic need to discover identity in difference without which experience becomes chaos" (p. 84). Chaos, to some extent, is a function of space that has not yet been ordered and therefore cannot be thought about. The drive to create order in the external world may be seen as reciprocal to the ordering of the inner world in a complex interplay between the ability to tolerate chaos and to also derive order within it, as we discover the familiar in the unfamiliar. This discovery requires "an ability to tolerate a temporary loss of sense of self, a temporary giving up of the discriminating ego which stands apart and tries to see things objectively and rationally and without emotional colouring" (Milner, 1952, p. 97). The ability to "lose one's self" in the moment is both a fundamental aspect of the creative act itself and also a mode whereby the product can be deeply appreciated.

Much as the earliest transformative experiences occur through the reverie of the mother, later creative acts require the internal capacity for reverie, made possible by a setting in which we are freed of the necessity for vigilance (Milner, 1957). The mother's reverie and attunement become prototypes for our own ability to *be* with ourselves and to let go of any rigid distinctions between self and other. The act of attuning to our own inherent sense of rhythm brings us closer to the sources of our own creativity, thereby offering a sense of order and uniqueness of vision that is beyond anything we might intentionally plan with the conscious mind.

Creativity requires the relatively free interplay of unconscious and conscious processes: phantasy and thinking, symmetry and asymmetry. Most fundamentally, art is a personal process, derived from moments of being. Milner (1957) described the "work of art, whatever its content, [as] . . . an externalization, through its shapes and lines and colours, of the unique psycho-physical rhythm of the person making it" (p. 230). This unique rhythm is one source of the vitality of a work of art, along with that derived from the union of artist and medium. This is the power of implicit knowledge, when we are so familiar with the process that we can be totally present within it, rather than having to think about it.

In some ways, this union with the medium may represent both an accommodation to, and a denial of, one's essential aloneness. One impetus toward creative endeavors may be, in part, the longing for a return to or merger with the original unity of self and other we experience in the womb and also, optimally, in the early experiences of union and reunion with the mother. The idealized relationship between self and other has its roots in what has been described as the "interactive awe" between mother and child (Grotstein, 1998).

In the absence of the mother's containing functions, the young child is at the mercy of forces beyond his capacity to tolerate or control. This deficit results in defensive avoidance or repetitive yearnings for reunion with the perfect mother. Milner (1950) suggested that the child moves from the mother as an idealized love object to the medium, which is more accommodating to his own needs and whims. "What the artist idealizes primarily is his medium. He is in love with it; . . . if he loves it enough so that he submits himself to its real qualities, at the same time as imposing his will upon it, the finished product may eventually justify the idealization" (p. 151).

Optimally, the creative endeavor becomes a way of moving beyond an unresolvable need for some perfect other, to creating a source of containment within the self through one's work. In this way, the work of art may be seen, paradoxically, as both an affirmation of the self as solitary and not needful, and also as an opportunity to be "found," in affirmation of that very need for the other. This duality is enacted through the capacity to create symbols for the expression of the inner life: the creation of new objects both denies and fills our need. For the audience, too, there is this paradox, in that we often experience both an affinity toward and a distancing from a work. At best, we are caught between the experience of "finding" and "being found" versus whatever distances us sufficiently to enable the experience to be more than a mere symbiotic interlude. Ultimately, it is the juxtaposition of the anomalous with the familiar that captures us, pushing us toward new and more profound integrations.

The artistic process is one whereby what Bollas (1987) has referred to as the "unthought known" can be formally represented and thereby known. What is fundamentally *self* becomes externalized in a way that potentially makes it more than self *or* other, in this way taking on some aspect of the universal. This dialectic between the particular and the universal, between discrete events and overarching meanings, gives art its plasticity (Rose, 1980). The interplay of the familiar and unfamiliar enhances our ability to perceive the underlying structure or meaning through the use of metaphors that expand meanings and heighten our appreciation of them. The metaphoric relationship introduces a creative space within which one can "play" with ideas (Winnicott, 1971).

FINDING ONE'S VOICE: AFFIRMING ONE'S VISION

The blocking of creativity is often a function of a deficit in regard to this capacity to play with ideas. Play requires the ability to be in touch with both our more loving and our more destructive aspects. According to Winnicott (1971), the capacity to be creative is nurtured in early experiences of playing at both creation and destruction. We can see this in the early "peek-a-boo" games, in which the child plays with the idea of creating and de-creating other and self. It also derives from the child's ability to be distressed and angry: to attack the mother and to know that she will survive. In this way, we come to understand that we can have an impact on our surroundings, but that the effects of this impact need not be disastrous. Perhaps more important, we learn that we can create, destroy, and re-create the subjective object (Grotstein, 2000c). Encountering and deconstructing limits is an inherent aspect of growth, much as fragmentation of meaning is crucial for any new understanding. Our comfort in both the power of the self and the resilience of the other becomes the context in which we can play with ideas, feelings, and objects.

For individuals for whom this negotiation has not been made, it is difficult to create of one's self with impunity. There is often an expectation of encountering censure rather than pleasure in the eye of the other. This expectation may then become a recurrent, nightmarish reality, as the need to protect the self interferes with the ability to make contact. Our patients' narratives offer us portraits of "mother and child" and of self-in-relation, within which we unravel layers of what it means to be with self and other for that individual.

This dilemma has been an important theme in my work with Elena, who had been a gifted composer in her earlier years, the recipient of several prestigious awards. Suddenly, her primary pleasure in creating music was gone, replaced by the burden of "performance." Elena's fears of rejection by, and sense of being repugnant to, her mother had made it impossible for her to create freely and, eventually, even to listen to music. Elena has spent many years trying to regain what was lost or, alternatively, to renounce her creative strivings. When she finally entered my door, she had slim hopes and huge reservations about trying, once again, to find in analysis something that had eluded her for 30 years. The ostensible reason for referral was an artistic block. The underlying reason was a chasm that had been created over time between this woman's ability to use her creative talents, and a fear and self-loathing that had become incapacitating and dehumanizing.

Our early hours were punctuated by a barrage instructing me as to what "the problem" was and was not; what she needed and did not. This barrage largely took the form of a diatribe against her most recent therapist, who had neither heard nor seen her. This misreading of Elena and her words had become, in the moment, an annihilation of self so profound that Elena had spent years trying to convince that therapist of the reality of her own subjective experience.

I became the recipient of the anger and fear, the anguish and despair. Through my countertransference reactions to this barrage, I was able to develop a picture of what might have occurred between Elena and her therapist, which was also a picture of what had occurred between Elena and her mother. She seemed to be telling me not to try to fix her problem: that the problem was more obdurate and unyielding than any solution could possibly be. And yet, she was coming to me for assistance. What was she needing from me? Certainly, my understanding. However, understanding was not enough, as she would tell me in no uncertain terms. Caring was certainly not enough. Caring was treacherous. It led to relaxing one's guard and opening one's self to further devastation.

The key must be whether or not I could actually comprehend what she was trying to tell me. We both had a stake in solving this dilemma. I, from my side, desperately wanted to understand sufficiently that I might be released from the energied attacks on me. And yet, hour after hour, she would try to get across to me exactly how awful her experience had been. With each new onslaught, I wondered what made her keep trying to tell me something I thought I had already heard.

Meanwhile, I was telling her about what I *was* hearing, seeing, and feeling. I played back to her the repugnance on her face as she talked about her mother's reaction to her. Elena seemed to be trying to create the (m)other she needed, much as Fairbairn (1952) described how we absorb the toxic aspect of the parent in our attempts to purify and "redeem" them (see Grotstein, 2000d). Then a new vista opened: as Elena began to see how she had pushed away anyone who was "like her" because of this self-repugnance that she carried with her, but which had remained unknown to her in any usable way. I was giving her a picture of a mother/therapist who had reached the limits of her capacity—who had no more to give. This possibility had not occurred to Elena: she had assumed that if she could just do it/say it right, the mother/therapist would then be able to give her what she needed and yearned for. It had not occurred to her that the other might be more limited than she.

This would seem to be one dilemma of the gifted individual in the hands of an unseeing, unyielding other, amplified by the societal tendency to depict the woman as other (Charles, forthcoming). Much of Elena's difficulty at the hands of psychoanalysis came from this sense of otherness: although Freud was in some sense respectful of the limits of his knowledge, the view of woman as "other" took on a life of its own. This dilemma was recapitulated in Elena's previous analyst's inability to truly hear what Elena was trying to tell her: "I can't accommodate to your 'truth' at present." Elena was saying in desperation, "You must accept me where I am."

For Elena, this lack of recognition was experienced as a rejection of essential facets of her being. As Klein (1946) has noted, repudiated aspects of self become persecutors, terrorizing us by their very existence. Part of what had kept Elena imprisoned was her inability to grapple with the fundamental rejection she had experienced in being reviled by her mother for reminding her of her own failures. This revulsion was perceived by Elena as an admonition to not be herself, to be other: an accommodation the mother appeared to have made. Elena could not fathom being other and hence became lost to herself.

Elena wonders that no one has ever heard her. It isn't support or caring she finds in me: "Your eyes aren't these luminous pools of warmth I fall into," she tells me. "It's that there's a mind in there. . . . I needed some help in solving my problems. But no one ever really heard me before."

Part of Elena's problem is that there is too much of a mind in there and that the demands she makes on herself and others are quite stringent. What seems to have been missing in previous treatments, I suggested to her, was the idea on either of their parts that there was a mismatch; that the other person really was not following her. If the therapist had known that and could have acknowledged it, they might have been able to find one another: Elena might have been seen. If Elena had been able to see it, she might have been able to avoid falling. However, with no one to know, to see, she would be invited to walk the tightrope once again; being assured that the safety net was surely in place; only to fall once more, with no acknowledgment that there had been a net missing, or a trap laid.

For Elena, the salient dilemma had been that there was no one waiting to affirm her reality. This absence is particularly perplexing as Elena is willing to engage in seeing: she is not only willing to point out the failures of the other, but also to engage actively in wondering about her own part. In fact, she is most interested in her *own* failures, which, she notes, are more under her control than those of the other. Her assumption has always been that the other is "OK": she just needs to figure out how to work with him or her. However, the other has always seemed alien, too remote to comprehend.

"You have been like a bridge," she said one day. "You see what's missing."

I have been willing to speak to what I see, as well. Elena's fear and anger are difficult to speak into, an aspect of herself that she had not been aware of. She was notably unaware of the power of her intensity, which impeded her ability to make sense of her interactions with important others in ways that might move beyond the impasses co-constructed out of hurt, ignorance, and fear.

In turn, Elena is beginning to see what has been missing and to speak to it, as well. She recounted to me an incident with her mother that highlighted the dilemma they have been caught in for all these years. Her mother mentioned in passing an important family event that Elena had missed because she had not been told about it. "Why didn't you tell me?" Elena had asked. "It didn't matter that you weren't there," replied her mother, reassuring her own concerns and completely missing those of her daughter. However, Elena was no longer accepting her mother's lack of responsiveness as a sign that Elena had nothing of value to say. Rather than becoming silenced, Elena kept trying to get back to her own point: to be recognized.

"It's not important," said the mother, finally, in exasperation, trying to move on to whatever point she had had in mind. "It's important to *me*," countered Elena. Her mother began to remonstrate Elena for always blaming her for everything. "It's not a matter of *blame*," replied Elena. "I'm *disappointed* that I wasn't able to have been there. I would have *liked* to have *been* there."

The following day Elena's mother called to relate an anecdote that had occurred between her and her granddaughter. The point of the anecdote was that she had pushed aside a request of the granddaughter's, not realizing that it mattered. "Please sit by me," the child had said. "No, you should be sitting with your father," replied the grandmother. "I'll sit behind you."

"I should have sat by her," said Elena's mother, "but I don't always get it at the time." This statement reverberated profoundly for Elena. Within these words was acknowledgment of a mother who tried and failed, and of a daughter who was pushed away through ignorance and ineptitude rather than condemnation. Here was the recognition that Elena had sought for so long and thought she might never see. Tears streamed down her face for all that had come in between. "All that pain," she said. "All those years believing there was something so terribly horribly wrong with me. Things could have been so different." Along with the loss, there is hope; along with the pain comes possibility.

For Elena, this recognition occurred in the context of my recognition of her, which enabled her to recognize herself. In counterpoint, she also recognizes the other more fully, which lends a greater richness and satisfaction to her encounters. It also allows her to tolerate blindness when she encounters it, without becoming lost within it. This is the invitation offered by psychoanalysis: if one is willing to look beyond the given, if one is willing to see beyond the ostensible reality, greater truths may be revealed.

Psychoanalysis offers tools for unpacking the condensations of meanings that become lethal "truths," so that we need not blind ourselves to escape from the "sins" of the father, the mother, or the child. Through this work, Elena has become better able to recognize, enjoy, and work with the patterns that signify meanings that had been occluded by fear and self-loathing. This ability brings her closer to being able to once again become immersed within the patterned experience she most loves— music—without becoming hopelessly lost in it.

As Elena tells me what she has been learning from watching the parents of her students facilitate or obstruct their development, she recounts to me with wonder and with gratitude her recollections of my willingness to stay with her even in the face of her anger and resistance. Coming to see herself from my perspective has provided an opening within which to see anew old truths that had precluded growth or understanding. It also provided a means for being more fully the self that had been constrained by her own self-rejection.

The repugnance that had become linked to self via her internalizations of her mother's disdain had become a block to Elena's ability to play. As Elena came to be able to recognize herself without running away, many of her interpersonal and creative inhibitions lightened. She was finally able to begin to explore, utilize, and enjoy her creative gifts in a way that had been foreclosed for many years. Play requires sufficient distance to be able to engage and disengage: to have a sufficiently separate other with whom one can interact (Winnicott, 1971). Overwhelming affect intensifies and symmetrizes experience, making it difficult to keep in mind the meaningful distinctions that ground us in consensual as well as idiosyncratic realities. Without these groundings, play becomes private, and we may lose this ability to intercommunicate with self and other that nourishes creativity (Charles, 2002).

CONCLUSION

The original visual context within which we are found and differentiated is the mother's face. Winnicott (1971) suggested that what the baby sees when he looks into the mother's face is himself: "the mother is looking at the baby, *and what she looks like is related to what she sees there*" (p. 112). The baby sees a reflection of himself: a responsive face that is lit by enjoyment encourages the child's interest in and enjoyment of self, whereas, "If the mother's face is unresponsive, then a mirror is a thing to be looked at but not looked into" (p. 113). In that event, it is very difficult for the individual to be creative in an organic, transformational way. Often, as has been the case for Elena, analysis provides the individual with a new, more responsive mirror. Winnicott (1971) put it this way: "I like to think . . . that if I do this well enough the patient will find his or her own self, and will be able to exist and feel real. Feeling real is more than existing; it is finding a way to exist as oneself, and to relate to objects as oneself, and to have a self to retreat into for relaxation" (p. 117).

The parent who encourages the child to discover the world, while keeping the edges safe enough that the child does not become overwhelmed, is fostering the type of resiliency that enhances the capacity for creative thought and action. Creative blocks often have to do with an impasse between self and other, and between self and world, in which we cannot bring anything original of the self into the world out of fear of how it will be reflected in the eye of the other. The reverberations of this fear reach back into our earliest encounters with the distant or disapproving parent. One resolution of this fear comes through creating a context in which we are able to see the self and its products in a more receptive light.

This perspective helps us to resolve the dilemma of having to renounce our yearnings for the early oneness with the perfect mother. Whether these arose from failures in the original parent/child bonding, or from the child's ultimate need to give up the illusion that they alone fill this place in mother's eye, what is created is a new vision or a new formulation of the old vision that asserts, reframes, or partially resolves our dilemma. Milner (1950) put it this way:

> Everyone's task in the transition from childhood to adulthood clearly centres around this problem of finding a particular niche in the social world, of finding the gap or need in the social structure into which one can pour one's creative energies and find that they are wanted . . . perhaps in painting one does create one's own gap by deciding on the frame, both literally and metaphorically [p. 133].

An important part of the frame, for the artist, is his or her own experience of self and of world. As we try to find ourselves in others, we often lose sight of our own vision: our own essential capacities and creativity. Adrienne Rich (1978) speaks to this issue in a poem in which she affirms the importance of attending to one's own rhythms and of speaking in one's own voice:

> But there are times—perhaps this is one of them—
> when we have to take ourselves more seriously or die;
> when we have to pull back from the incantations,
> rhythms we've moved to thoughtlessly . . . .
>
> No one who survives to speak
> new language, has avoided this:
> the cutting-away of an old force that held her
> rooted to an old ground [pp. 74–75].

In her attempts to negotiate the dilemma of how we can bring our primary experience into our art, Rich stands with Ana Mendieta in affirming the importance of acknowledging our roots in the language of material reality—the body and land that ground it and give it life (see Figure 5.5). In this way, each affirms the importance of being able to know and value our own perspective, which is what we each uniquely have to offer. Creativity, ultimately, springs from the ability to affirm our own

Figure 5.5. Ana Mendieta, *Serie árbol de la vida* (Tree of Life Series), 1976. Color photograph of earth/body work with cloth and tree. 13¹/₄ × 20 inches; 33.7 × 50.8 cm. Galerie Lelong, New York. Courtesy of the Estate of Ana Mendieta and Galerie Lelong, New York.

experience in a way that transcends the personal, by speaking to others of the universal in a uniquely personal way. What may be most important about considering creativity from an analytic perspective is that it invites us to look deeper into our own experience and to affirm and elucidate the rhythms and patterns that make that experience both unique and universal. From this vantage point, we are in a better position to "recognize" the other (in Kris's [1952] terms) and to thereby participate in an act of co-creation that does not obscure self, but rather enables it to flourish.

6

THE LANGUAGE OF THE BODY: ALLUSIONS TO SELF-EXPERIENCE IN WOMEN'S POETRY

No one lives in this room
without confronting the whiteness of the wall
behind the poems, planks of books,
photographs of dead heroines.
Without contemplating last and late
the true nature of poetry. The drive
to connect. The dream of a common language.

　　　　　　　　　　　　　—Adrienne Rich,
　　　　　　"Origins and History of Consciousness"

*I*n analysis, we seek this common language with each patient, searching for profound truths that are relatively inaccessible to the conscious mind, through a journey enacted largely in the conscious/verbal domain. Many theorists, such as Ogden (1989), have noted the tendency to valorize the conscious integrative functions over more primary sensory awareness and yet there is also a deepening appreciation for the contributions of early sensory experiences—such as those associated with attunements in the mother/infant dyad—to the capacity to know self and other (Seligman, 1998, 1999). Bion (1962, 1963, 1965) extended our ability to understand how these primary experiences become transformed, through his explications of what he termed "transformations in 'O,'" in which we move from the "ultimate reality" as experienced (which is inherently unspeakable until transformed into symbols that can be communicated), toward a greater understanding of, or appreciation for, the "ultimate reality" as such (which is inherently unknowable [Bion, 1965]).

The paradox is that we must continually grapple with a reality that is outside of our ability to truly know and comprehend it, and yet our experience of knowing this reality may be quite profound, beyond anything we might come to know through other means. The capacity to *understand,* as Bion used the term, is built on the capacity to be present in our own experience. In this way, the woman would seem to bear a unique relation to O, in that the body so profoundly constrains and patterns her experiences of the world (Charles, 2000b). Even when we work within the more cerebral realms, we are reminded repeatedly of the impact of bodily constraints. From the regularities of the menstrual cycle, which ground us in the rhythmicity of time; to more striking occurrences, such as menarche, pregnancy, childbirth, and menopause, which ground us in the rhythmicity of the life cycle itself, we are reminded repeatedly—and sometimes abruptly and disjunctively—of the exigencies of time and space that locate us within the corporeal world. Love and loss, aging and illness bring other lights and shadows into our experiences of self.

Our earliest experience is derived of and through the body: from the moment of conception, physical sensations order our universe. Initially, there would seem to be little distinction between inside and out, an intimacy refound in later years in the feel of lying entwined with an other and not knowing their heartbeat from our own. In the early months of life, the mother metabolizes the child's experiences, ordering and giving meaning to them in accordance with her own. We are fed back imperfect mirrorings of self-experience, through which we must find our own language, sailing toward that difficult fissure between that which might be understood by the other without forsaking too much of self.

This interplay between self and other is optimally rooted in the primary self-experience that Winnicott (1960) described as "true self," with origins in our earliest sensations of vitality in "the aliveness of the body tissues and the workings of the body functions" (p. 148). Winnicott depicted the true self as an inborn potentiality—closely akin to our notions of "soul" and yet profoundly allied with self as body—thereby deconstructing the traditional dualism of mind versus body. This type of conception of the self is in accord with field theories, in which events are essentially and inherently interconnected (Kulka, 1997), and matter is both substance and energy. It is also profoundly in line with many women's experience of self.

In the art of many women, we can see attempts to articulate the language of the body, grounded in the senses and derived from the fundamental truths experienced through *being* (in the sense of Winnicott's [1971] use of the term) in the world. Truths of the body mirror truths of self and world, in an intricate interplay in a universe in which there are no clear boundaries between self and other, and one can profoundly "touch" an other without the necessity of physical contact (see chapter 4). Bion (1963) suggested that necessity creates the realization; certainly, for many poets, putting self-experience into words is one such necessity. Necessity may also dictate the forms by which we order and recount our experiences, in our attempts to understand both self and other.

The body would seem to be one essential form that defines, proscribes, and delimits our creations. A body of work often reflects the level of comfort the artist has achieved with her own body. Anne Sexton (1988), for example, seems to have spent a good deal of her life trying to escape from her body, an endeavor she finally succeeded in effecting, through suicide. In the work of Maya Angelou (1978), in contrast, we see a profound comfort, ease, and enjoyment of the body, as her words roll and ripple in sinuous pleasure. In spite of their ostensible dissimilarities, the poetry of each of these women is built on words drawn from the language of the body.

The often diametrically opposed forces of society and self encourage an ambivalent relationship with the body, impeding the ability to know and make use of primary sensations, such as affect. Affect serves as both a signal and an organizer of experience (Krystal, 1988) and is useful to the extent that its signal functions are appreciated. However, current western society pushes women to live outside of their bodily felt awareness, vilifying common sense by calling it "old wives' tales"; giving a pejorative tone to terms that allude to more primary understandings, such as "intuition"; and endorsing a view of the woman's body that opposes the actuality of woman's physiology and of natural development: reversing even our conceptions of development itself, by holding the body (and often the mind) of an immature child/woman as the ideal. The visible signs of having lived tend to be repudiated rather than respected, as we starve and cut and staple ourselves in search of an impossible, life-denying ideal. In this age of fast pace and overload, we have lost our grounding, as well as our respect for that which can only be known through grounding one's self in one's own experience. This is a truth of which many female poets, such as Adrienne Rich, struggle to remind us—a wisdom too easily overlooked or forgotten. However, for many women, being grounded in the body becomes a form of bondage, as exemplified in the work of Sylvia Plath (Axelrod, 1990).

The capacity to move beyond the experience as such, and to be able to play with ideas (Winnicott, 1971), is a function of our ability to attain a position of sufficient perspective from which to reflect on and make sense of the experience. In this regard, unconscious processes pose a particular challenge, in part because of their greater dimensionality (Matte-Blanco, 1988), the multiplicities of layerings and interconnections that so easily elude our conscious grasp. In our attempts to simplify our views, we tend to create a false world in which the two modes referred to as primary and secondary process, or as symmetrical versus asymmetrical domains of experience (Matte-Blanco, 1975, 1988), are dichotomized. This disjunction further impedes our efforts to make sense of self and experience, which requires an ability to integrate the more primary knowings that tend to be understood through similarities (symmetry), with the more elaborated understandings of the verbal, rational mind (Matte-Blanco, 1988). Poetry offers a unique opportunity to explore the interplay between these two modes in a way that enriches both.

Nonverbal and affective awareness tend to be characterized by a greater degree of symmetry, whereas the verbal domain tends to be characterized by greater distinctions between like things, thereby developing a system of categories whereby the world may be ordered. In poetry, our grounding in the printed page allows us to move from equivalency to equivalency through the medium of affect, which lends itself well to symmetrical experiences, in which distinctions tend to disappear. Affect is synergistic in nature, in that the greater the intensity, the more evocative it is of similar experiences associated with the same affect (Bucci, 1997b). Time and space are transcended, as affect draws together similar experiences through this common bond, while the form and structure of the poem give an edge to the experience, thereby containing it.

In this way, poetry juxtaposes the worlds of symmetry and asymmetry and brings us back to our more primary knowings in a way that integrates, and thereby transcends, the experience itself. These primary knowings are evocative of early experiences of symmetrization (Matte-Blanco, 1975) between self and other, in which there is little differentiation between the rhythms of mother and child (Anzieu, 1993). In these early experiences, there is at first a great deal of symmetrization or "psychic equivalence" (Fonagy and Target, 1997) of unlike things. Over time, we move from simple equations of symbol and object to greater distinctions between the symbol and that which is symbolized (Segal, 1957), in ongoing attempts to integrate internal and external realities.

Just as symbol formation moves from self-experience toward intercommunication, so too does the development of thought move from primary sensory experience toward greater elaboration. Klein (1957) affirmed the importance of attending to that which feels primitive within us, to be able to "revive fundamental situations . . . [or] 'memories in feeling' " (p. 234), in order to be able to develop sufficient perspective that one might perceive those experiences in some new way. In her explication of the intertwining modes of experience she refers to as "paranoid-schizoid" and "depressive," Klein pointed to an essential dialectic in which meaning is created, synthesized, broken apart once again, and expanded. This process enables us to reflect on our experience from a position of disjunction with the other. Asymmetry allows both historicity (Ogden, 1989) and a greater capacity for reflection, as disjunction invites us to see anew what had become invisible through habituation.

The capacity for reflective awareness underlies Bion's (1963) depictions of the processes by which sensory experience becomes transformed into verbal thought, largely based on the containing and metabolizing functions of the mother through reverie. At one extreme, we have the experience as such: "the sensation is, in itself, a primary experience, which is irreducible to description, though we constantly try to describe it. The same is true of symmetrical being: . . . it does not happen, but just is" (Matte-Blanco, 1975, p. 101). At the other extreme, we have the abstraction. Bion (1962) contrasted these two modes of understanding in his depictions of the development of thinking, noting the essential interplay between experience and abstraction. The concrete and particular ground the experience, thereby giving meaning to it, whereas "formalization and abstraction . . . have the effect, by removing the concrete and particular, of eliminating aspects that obscure the relationship of one element to another" (p. 52).

In his equivalence of formalization and abstraction, Bion obscured an essential difference: although formalization implies a greater level of abstraction than the thing-itself, it also implies a greater level of concreteness than the abstraction per se. Formalization implies the creation of form, but also the constraints of becoming defined in a particular form. The risk in formalization is that we might retain the form, but lose the essence. The risk in abstraction is that we might retain the essence without the type of grounding that might give it meaning or vitality. For some theorists, growth is "the generation of form" (Ingold, 1990, p. 215). Without the experience that underlies the abstraction, the form remains empty: it has no life.

The abstract and the concrete form a complex interrelationship that facilitates the elaboration of meaning in their interplay as, alternately, container and contained. The capacity to form abstractions enables us to build on our experiences in a way that brings greater understanding and facilitates communication. However, at times it is the capacity to enact what has eluded verbal understanding that grounds us in our own reality, thereby facilitating communication and bringing us closer to the understanding we seek (Kumin, 1996). Poetry would seem to be one such type of enactment that at times bypasses the realm of asymmetrical knowledge, to enter our awareness in a much more primary fashion, through our more intuitive nonverbal channels (see Trevarthen, 1995).

Psychoanalysis has traditionally been framed in terms of verbal understandings. However, many analysts, such as Bion (1965), have noted the paradox that transformations do not occur solely in verbal form: verbal knowing can actually impede one's ability to be in a different place with one's self. "Knowing about" can obfuscate the experience as lived, thereby precluding real understanding. Art provides a means for translating primary awareness into patterned form, which can then be utilized as a way of discovering self.

The quest to find one's own voice has been a particularly difficult one for women, in which the woman's voice has been disparaged and devalued (Le Doeuff, 1987). It is hard to even imagine what "women's writing" might look like if freed from the bounds of patriarchy (see, for example, Marks and de Courtivron, 1981). Perhaps the tendency to depreciate the woman may be due, at least in part, to our terror of being engulfed by the mother, which encourages us to keep her primary knowings at bay. And yet, in depreciating ourselves, valuable information is lost: putting the self forward is an important means for understanding. The echoes we receive in response give us crucial information as to our relative place, safety, and meanings in the world. Much of these negotiations occur implicitly rather than explicitly, as we develop what Stern et al. (1998) have called "implicit relational knowing." The more primary, nonverbal systems tend to function more efficiently when we do not impose order through the more conscious, rational mind.

Poetry is a unique medium in that it is built upon nonverbal understandings using the medium of words. It should be noted, however, that even though the medium is words, nonverbal aspects—such as placement and intonation—establish rhythms whose meanings interact importantly with the more explicit content. Readers tend to respond to recurrent patterns in literary texts, rather than to the content per se (Miall and Kuiken, 1994). This tendency results in idiosyncratic readings: "Experienced readers will begin to anticipate the recurrence and development of certain affective meanings, perhaps only in imprecise intuitions at first, but increasingly explicitly as these recurrences accumulate" (Miall and Kuiken, 1994, p. 349). These types of foregrounding processes (departures from normal language in terms of rhythm, phrase structure, and word usage) invite the reader's attention and feelings of engagement (Miall and Kuiken, 1994). Anomaly encourages affective, idiosyncratic responses (Miall, 1987), consistent with Coleridge's (1817) view that art enhances one's ability to see anew what one had ceased noticing by force of habit. In this way, literary texts "enable us to reflect on our own commitments and concerns: to discover better what they are, to reconfigure them, to place the ideas about our aims and identity in a different perspective" (Miall and Kuiken, 1994, p. 351).

For many artists, the creative endeavor is both an assertion of self and an act of self-discovery, whereby meanings can be considered, elucidated, and transformed. It is a way of knowing while not-knowing—revealing important truths while also obscuring them sufficiently to tolerate the exposure. In this way, it can

serve the same function for the audience: providing an opportunity to know important aspects of self and yet to keep them
safely at bay as other, when necessary.

Literary texts tend to invite subtle bodily involvement,
through the use of what Lakoff (1987) termed "natural metaphors."
Both Sylvia Plath and Adrienne Rich use this type of metaphor
to engage the reader kinesthetically, thereby encouraging the
reader to become present within the text. In this way, as Plath
and Rich explore their own truths about self-experience, they
invite the reader to do the same. For Plath, these explorations
have a bound quality. For example, in her poem "Three
Women," Plath (1972) considers pregnancy and childbirth as
experiences within which the women become bound and cap-
tured. There is a sense that there is little control; perhaps only
the possibility of survival at some cost to self. In contrast, in
Rich's poems, we encounter a similar preoccupation with self-
experience and with the profound impact it has on the person,
but there seems to be a greater possibility for transformation,
in the positive sense in which Bion (1965) used the term.

WHEN GROUNDING BECOMES BONDAGE: THE WORK OF SYLVIA PLATH

In Sylvia Plath's (1972) poem "Three Women: A Poem for Three
Voices," she speaks from primary self-experience in the act of
creation. Using the frames of three disparate women who each
stand at the uneasy precipice of motherhood, Plath expresses
her own ambivalence and multiplicity in the three voices that
speak within the text. The woman of the first voice is largely at
one with her experience. She feels enlarged and enlivened by
her pregnancy:

> When I walk out, I am a great event.
> I do not have to think, or even rehearse.
> What happens in me will happen without attention
>
> [Plath, 1972, p. 47].

This woman carries life within her, and with it a new life for herself. Although she is enlivened, she is also frightened. She wonders what will be left of her as this new life supervenes on her own; there is the sense that life, as she knows it, may end:

> I am dumb and brown. I am a seed about to break.
> The brownness is my dead self, and it is sullen:
> It does not wish to be more, or different.
> Dusk hoods me in blue now, like a Mary.
> O color of distance and forgetfulness!—
> When will it be, the second when Time breaks
> And eternity engulfs it, and I drown utterly?
>
> [Plath, 1972, p. 51].

Eternity intervenes; becoming mother is equated with both losing and finding self. When her child is born, this woman is amazed and frightened by the vastness of the task before her. She would like to wall off the world in order to protect her child (and self), but realizes the futility of even trying, and assuages her fears by replacing the nightmarish images that have haunted her with the reassurance of the fully normal child (self?) she has borne. She disowns potential disappointments and affirms her determination to bring her own vision of this child into actuality:

> I am reassured. I am reassured. . . .
>
> I am simple again. I believe in miracles.
> I do not believe in those terrible children
> Who injure my sleep with their white eyes, their finger-
>   less hands.
> They are not mine. They do not belong to me.
>
> I shall meditate upon normality. . . .

I do not will him to be exceptional.
It is the exception that interests the devil.
It is the exception that climbs the sorrowful hill
Or sits in the desert and hurts his mother's heart
[Plath, 1972, pp. 61–62].

In this way, the child is conceived as an affirmation of the mother, as the mother creates the child in her own image, thereby invoking the false self.

For the woman of the second voice, even more strikingly, the new life being created within her is de-creating her. She carries death; the death of her child becomes her own. For this woman, the images are cold, empty, and barren in a world in which she can find no home, much as her child could find no home within her. She feels helpless and useless, in a world in which she is constrained by forces within and without:

It is a world of snow now. I am not at home
[Plath, 1972, p. 50].

She, too, is overtaken by forces beyond her control, as the moon moves her to no good end:

It is she that drags the blood-black sea around
Month after month, with its voices of failure.
I am helpless as the sea at the end of her string.
I am restless. Restless and useless. I, too, create corpses
[Plath, 1972, p. 55].

After her miscarriage, the woman of the second voice readies herself, a bit unsteady, to go back to her life as though nothing has happened. She is consumed by the nothing that has happened, that has de-created her in its path. She hopes against all hope to deny that it matters, thereby de-realizing both body and self:

And so I stand, a little sightless. So I walk
Away on wheels, instead of legs, they serve as well.
And learn to speak with fingers, not a tongue.
The body is resourceful.
The body of a starfish can grow back its arms
And newts are prodigal in legs. And may I be
As prodigal in what lacks in me. . . .

I am myself again. There are no loose ends.
I am bled white as wax, I have no attachments.
I am flat and virginal, which means nothing has
   happened,
Nothing that cannot be erased, ripped up and
   scrapped, begun again

[Plath, 1972, pp. 58–59].

The woman of the second voice affirms her determination to
move forward, as though nothing had ever happened: to deny
the enormity of that which has taken place within her body and
being. However, she cannot de-create her child without de-creating the body/self that had sought to give it life. De-realized
and de-personalized, she confronts the empty image of self:

This woman who meets me in windows—she is neat.

So neat she is transparent, like a spirit. . . .
She is deferring to reality.
It is I. It is I—
Tasting the bitterness between my teeth.
The incalculable malice of the everyday

[Plath, 1972, p. 60].

As she goes back home, this woman is faced, once again, with
the reality she had tried to escape. Although she braces herself
against the pain of it, life begins again. In the prickles of awak-
ening, like a limb too long unused, she begins to move back into

her experience, much as life emerges in the bleak surround, through the cracks in the pavement:

> Safe on the mattress, hands braced, as for a fall.
> I find myself again. I am no shadow . . .
> The city waits and aches. The little grasses
> Crack through stone, and they are green with life
> [Plath, 1972, p. 64].

The woman of the third voice is not ready for that other being created within herself, and yet feels powerless to stop this process. She dissociates the love she feels for the child, though, somewhat disjunctively, she also seems aware that the child thrives in it.

> I wasn't ready.
> I had no reverence.
> I thought I could deny the consequence—
> But it was too late for that. It was too late, and the face
> Went on shaping itself with love, as if I was ready
> [Plath, 1972, p. 49].

The woman of the third voice seeks to obliterate the reality of the child she had carried inside, as she hears her through the glass and tries to avoid being caught by the sounds of her cries. She wants to distance herself from her child and yet, in her imagination she envisions her:

> I see her in my sleep, my red, terrible girl. . . .
> Her cries are hooks that catch and grate like cats.
> It is by these hooks she climbs to my notice.
> She is crying at the dark, or at the stars
> That at such a distance from us shine and whirl
> [Plath, 1972, p. 56].

She is a small island, asleep and peaceful,
And I am a white ship hooting: Goodbye, goodbye.

. . . There is an emptiness.
I am so vulnerable suddenly.
I am a wound walking out of hospital.
I am a wound that they are letting go.
I leave my health behind. I leave someone
Who would adhere to me: I undo her fingers like
    bandages: I go
                         [Plath, 1972, p. 59].

The woman of the third voice speaks of the terrible emptiness that has taken up residence inside, as though it has overtaken and engulfed her. The emptiness becomes her: she is all
wound and vulnerability, as she wrenchingly leaves behind the
child who clings to her spirit and will not let go. She tries to take
up her own life once again, but the emptiness is profound:

Today the colleges are drunk with spring.
My black gown is a little funeral:
It shows I am serious.
The books I carry wedge into my side.
I had an old wound once, but it is healing.
I had a dream of an island, red with cries.
It was a dream, and did not mean a thing
                         [Plath, 1972, p. 61].

In denying her child, the woman of the third voice denies
her self in a move toward not-knowing. She is unable to integrate the loss, but rather loses both body and self in her denial.
As time passes, absence figures into her depiction of the world
around her, and yet she seems to have no awareness of it, only
a vague sense of absence become self. In her final musings, there
is an interplay of unconscious awareness with conscious denial;
she carries her child with her as absence, in her images of the
world. Absence becomes the lens that patterns her universe:

Hot noon in the meadows. The buttercups
Swelter and melt, and the lovers
Pass by, pass by.
They are black and flat as shadows.
It is so beautiful to have no attachments!
I am solitary as grass. What is it I miss?
Shall I ever find it, whatever it is?

The swans are gone. Still the river
Remembers how white they were.
It strives after them with its lights.
It finds their shapes in a cloud.
What is that bird that cries
With such sorrow in its voice?
I am young as ever, it says. What is it I miss?
[Plath, 1972, pp. 62–63].

In Plath's poem, the woman's experience of self becomes patterned by the body so profoundly that she is, at times, unable to know self, other, or world. In this poem, there is an interplay between body and self, as the mothers attempt to translate body experience into knowledge that can be integrated toward self-understanding, without becoming overwhelmed by that understanding. Plath depicts the tensions between self and creation, self and other, as instantiated within the flesh in the tension between the mother and her images of her child. In contrast, other female poets, such as Adrienne Rich, would seem to have made a greater peace with the body, from which perspective they are better able to integrate what are often seen as essential dualisms of the human dilemma.

TRANSFORMATIONS IN "O"

Bion (1965) addressed these fundamental dualisms in his depictions of "O" (ultimate reality) versus "K" (knowledge, inevitably constrained). The two manifestations of O—as primary experience versus ultimate reality—bear a striking resemblance to views of god in which the individual is seen as a manifestation of the infinite, closely akin to Coleridge's (1817) view of the poem as a manifestation of a greater truth than might be accessible through intentional thought. The infant would seem to experience O as a kind of "natural language" (Grotstein, personal communication, June, 1999) before it becomes altered and transformed into symbolic language whereby the natural language becomes lost. The mother's translation of the child's experiences, to the extent that it is imperfect, results in bizarre (unusable; unintegratable) objects, which are often also "civilized" objects. The baby learns a language for communicating to others about self and to self about both self and other that will, of the necessity born of the imperfection of the original translation, move further and further away from the original experience. In this way, knowledge, as learned, comes to obfuscate and preclude understanding, as experienced. And yet, to the extent that the translation has been into "civilized objects," there will be the illusion of understanding between people who have suffered similar mistranslations.

Even when the translations are imperfect, they do affirm that translation/transformation is possible, thereby encouraging the type of self-reflection that can help us to rediscover aspects of the nonverbal self that have eluded conscious awareness. Primary experience becomes the basis for what Bion (1965) has depicted as "transformations in O," as the thing-in-itself is transformed into practical symbolic knowledge (K). This interplay between the experience-as-such of the paranoid-schizoid position and the greater reflectivity of the depressive position highlights what current infant researchers are finding to be a crucial marker of a secure sense of self—which Main (1995) described as the ability to reflect coherently on one's experiences and Fonagy and his colleagues (1995) described as "reflective self-functioning"—derived from early resonances between mother and child.

Grotstein (personal communication, June 1999) suggested that "we must make 'O' personal and subjective in order to have a sense of realness, agency and purpose, as well as identity. Thus, there are two O's, the impersonal and the one we make personal for ourselves, the content of the unconscious." Following this line of thought, the impersonal becomes personal through its registrations upon the senses. However, in this form it is unknowable without being transformed by consensual understanding. Originally, the mother's reverie provides this transformative power; over time, we learn to perform this function for ourselves. In this way, O is always both personal and impersonal; we would seem to real-ize the impersonal/personal nature of O through the medium of the transpersonal.

To live in a world in which transformation is possible is to maintain the possibility of transformations toward O, rather than inevitably away. To the extent that the mother can truly keep the baby "in mind," the translating function may be consistent enough with the infant's experience to become an evolution back to O (assuming that O must reflect a "true" state of affairs within the individual's experience, which is also a reflection of a true state of affairs outside any particular experience, which we try to know but cannot fathom without particularizing it). These congruent translations affirm primary experience, thereby also affirming the value and reliability of the "true self," an important underpinning for any real meeting with an other.

O is inherently beyond the self, and yet our experience of O is always through the self, and therefore of the self. Grotstein (personal communication, June 1999) spoke evocatively of rendering its "non-humanness and indifference into personal terms of our personality with which we can survive and live." The transformation for the infant would seem to be of the *ineffable,* which becomes distorted in the process; to the *contained version,* which can only speak of it, and therefore only approximate it; toward the *original experience,* which becomes more than the original experience, itself, by virtue of its having become known in whatever capacity (as long as the knowing is not so much a denial of that which is becoming known that we can no longer find O).

These are elusive truths. Much as analysts have searched for a dynamic model through which to understand conceptions of the unconscious, unbounded by the conventions of time and space, so, too, do poets explore these realms in their medium that is, explicitly, outside the bounds of normal speech. Poetry is a particularly apt medium to communicate these types of truths, because it is both of language and beyond language. "Poetry attempts to convey something beyond what can be conveyed in prose rhythms" (Eliot, 1943, p. 23). It moves beyond the surface text to include rhythm and structure as fundamental derivatives of meaning (Miall and Kuiken, 1994). This is the type of multidimensional process that profoundly informs our understanding of self and world and yet that we have particular difficulty conceptualizing (Matte-Blanco, 1975). Poetry offers us a medium in which to play with dimensionality through the frames of time and space, which can merge and be disjoined through the placement of the words on the pages and the contexts in which they are framed. In this way, the more primary aspects of experience can be communicated through less explicit means, such as rhythm, tone, and prosody.

INTEGRATING BODY AND SPIRIT: THE WORK OF ADRIENNE RICH

Poetry is one means for attempting to portray the ineffable: that which we can know, but cannot easily communicate in normal speech. In the poetry of many women, we can see this struggle to bring primary self-experience into the world in ways in which it might be received by an other, without distorting it beyond recognition. Adrienne Rich is one poet whose work would seem to embody the ongoing conflict between body becoming mind and mind becoming body in ways that speak profoundly of the woman's experience of self as constrained by body and yet as also manifested in body. Rich (1981) speaks of this dilemma in her poem "For Memory":

> that common life we each and all bent out of orbit from
> to which we must return simply to say
> *this is where I came from*
> *this is what I knew . . .*

freedom is daily, prose-bound, routine
remembering. Putting together, inch by inch
the starry worlds. From all the lost collections

[p. 22].

In this poem, Rich juxtaposes the universal and the particular, creating one from the other in a dizzying dance from which she rescues us, only to set us adrift once again. This is a repetitive theme in the volume *The Dream of a Common Language,* in which Rich (1978) writes poignantly of the move from the oneness of being to the particular manifestation: from the oneness of union to the stark isolation of separateness. For example, in the poem "Sibling Mysteries" she writes:

words flash from you I never thought of
we are translations into different dialects

of a text still being written
in the original

yet our eyes drink from each other
our lives were driven down the same dark canal

[Rich, 1978, p. 51].

Bion (1962) described this same process of estrangement and reunion, as we move from a sense of primary union to the particularization of self that defines us. He used as an illustration of this primal dilemma the Tower of Babel story, in which there is the presumption of understanding until the awareness of disjunction shatters the sense of oneness, leaving us unalterably, essentially, alone. Bion (1963) noted how in this story, similar to the oedipal myth, moving toward knowledge is forbidden and punished ruthlessly. In making the important distinction between moving toward knowing and moving away from it, Bion referred to "alpha function" (primary mentation) in terms of an awareness of patternings, which may or may not be verbal in nature. The primary sense impression, as thing-in-itself, undigested and unelaborated (the original O), becomes linked with other experiences. In this way, primary experience becomes patterned in ways that are meaningful and yet these meanings may be relatively inaccessible to the conscious mind.

As we vacillate between our desires to know and to not-know, pattern is often a key to understanding. For example, poetry, as a form, is built upon the patterning of elements and the interplay of meanings. "Poetic language insistently conveys the underlying physicality of thought. It is reflected in the weight, texture, and motoric rhythm of words against silences" (Rose, 1984, p. 22). Our willingness to sit with the language of the body encourages the relatively free interplay between the levels of conscious and unconscious and between verbal and nonverbal ways of knowing, facilitating metaphoric understanding. The metaphoric relationship moves us to a level of abstraction that creates a distance between the reality referred to and the mode of expression, making it easier to think about each, as well as the relationship between the two. In this way, it introduces the transitional space and facilitates the ability to play with ideas (Winnicott, 1963, 1971), to see anew that which had become obscured by familiarization (Miall and Kuiken, 1994).

Bion (1963) depicted the recursive nature of the connections between the paranoid-schizoid and the depressive positions —by which the verbal informs the nonverbal and vice-versa—as a dialectic between our essential aloneness and our essential oneness. He suggested that we move toward resolution of this dilemma in the continuing interplay between fragmentation (the paranoid-schizoid position) and metabolization/integration (the depressive position). The paranoid-schizoid position is characterized by discontinuities in experiences, whereby the fragmentation of old meanings enables us to break through rigid boundaries and envision new possibilities, which can then become integrated into a larger whole. In poetry, fragmentation occurs through the patternings of words and lines on the page; the breaks and gaps confront us with novel and more personal readings of the text, which inform our interpretations and integrations of the material (Miall and Kuiken, 1994). In this way, fragmentation and integration serve as container and contained for one another in a continuing interplay in which each is essential for any real growth or understanding.

In the poem "A Vision," Rich (1981) plays with the theme of knowing and not-knowing: more specifically, the terror of knowing self:

What is your own will that it
can so transfix you
why are you forced to take this test
over and over and call it God
why not call it you and get it over

you with your hatred of enforcement
and your fear of blinding?

[pp. 50–51].

This passage would also seem to speak to the movement from the primary experience as O to the universal experience of O, the movement from becoming self to becoming god that Bion (1970) has described as the role of the "mystic." The mystic "needs to reassert a direct experience of god of which he has been, and is, deprived by the institutionalized group" (Bion, 1970, p. 77). For Bion, the mystic intrudes on the complacency of the larger society, thereby potentially enriching and enlivening those she touches (Charles, 2001e). This is also the role of the poet, whereby the particular provides an opportunity for the reader to experience the universal through the invocation of the personal.

Rich is a master at inviting us into these explorations of the sensory experience of primary knowings. In the poem "Planetarium," (1968), she (Rich, 1984) describes feeling assaulted by the infinite, as well as by the necessity to derive meanings from the multitude of messages in a universe inherently unfathomable:

I have been standing all my life in the
direct path of a battery of signals
the most accurately transmitted most
untranslateable language in the universe
I am a galactic cloud so deep   so invo-
luted that a light wave could take 15
years to travel through me   And has
taken   I am an instrument in the shape
of a woman trying to translate pulsations
into images   for the relief of the body
and the reconstruction of the mind

[p. 116].

In the preceding passage, Rich evocatively juxtaposes the necessity and the impossibility of translating one's self with any accu-
racy into something that might communicate its essence. In her
encounters with the ineffable, Rich is not unchanged: she struggles, in her reverie, to metabolize these bits of experience into
meaningful elements from which she might derive a more
cogent narrative.

Rich is exquisitely aware of the patternings that become
imprinted into our beings via primary experience. In "Shooting
Script," she (Rich, 1984) describes these patterns through which
self becomes known, contained, and constrained:

Of simple choice they are the villagers; their clothes
     come with
them like red clay roads they have been walking.

The sole of the foot is a map, the palm of the hand a
     letter,
learned by heart and worn close to the body.

They seemed strange to me, till I began to recall their
     dialect

[p. 140].

This is the "unthought known" (Bollas, 1987): those primary experiences that elude our more conscious, cognitive attempts at understanding, but rather must be approached intuitively, through our more implicit awarenesses of nonverbal patterned meanings.

Rich speaks of how patterning becomes self, patterning each thought, each movement: our whole way of understanding and being in the world. And yet she also defies this patterning, speaking of the ambivalence we experience in being human, and how this ambivalence at times brings us to try to deny our selves and our destinies, thereby obscuring from us our own capacities. In "Power," she (Rich, 1978) writes of the ironic tragedy of Marie Curie:

> she must have known she suffered   from radiation
>   sickness
> her body bombarded for years   by the element
> she had purified
> It seems she denied to the end
> the sources of the cataracts on her eyes
> the cracked and suppurating skin   of her finger-ends
> til she could no longer hold   a test-tube or a pencil
>
> She died   a famous woman   denying
> her wounds
> denying
> her wounds   came   from the same source as her
>   power

[p. 3].

Note how the spaces come to carry meanings—they disrupt the flow by which we carry ourselves forward, somewhat unconsciously, and startle us into thinking more pointedly about the meanings of these pauses. In this way, Rich forces us to take account of the silence. This silence, or absence of voice, is an important theme for artists (Loeb and Podell, 1995), and most

particularly for women artists, for whom the voice has been devalued or remained unarticulated (Le Doeuff, 1987).

There is a power in silence, but also a submission. This dilemma
has concerned Rich for some time, as she has struggled with the
lie that is often implicit in the woman's silence (Rich, 1979). Rich
(1978) expands on this theme in a poem entitled "Hunger," in
which she touches on her ideas of women's power and how it tends
to become subverted, a recurrent theme in her work:

> I stand convicted by all my convictions—
> you, too. We shrink from touching
> our power, we shrink away, we starve ourselves
> and each other, we're scared shitless
> of what it could be to take and use our love,
> hose it on a city, on a world,
> to wield and guide its spray, destroying
> poisons, parasites, rats, viruses—
> like the terrible mothers we long and dread to be
>   [p. 13].

This would seem to be the other side of O—the part that terri-
fies us and keeps us from our own source; the part that knows
we are both love and hate, wound and healing touch. Creativity
is fed by the capacity to play with both creation and destruction
(Winnicott, 1971), a motif to which Rich (1978) returns in Verse
XX of "Twenty-One Love Poems":

> That conversation we were always on the edge
> of having, runs on in my head,
> at night the Hudson trembles in New Jersey light
> polluted water yet reflecting even
> sometimes the moon
> and I discern a woman
> I loved, drowning in secrets, fear wound round her
>   throat
> and choking her like hair. And this is she

with whom I tried to speak, whose hurt, expressive
    head
turning aside from pain, is dragged down deeper
where it cannot hear me,
and soon I shall know I was talking to my own soul
                                                    [p. 35].

This is another recurrent theme for Rich: how we try to find
self through other and to find other through self. In this endeavor,
images of the body evoke primary sensations and affective experiences associated with being lost and being found. There is a particular poignancy to this theme in the work of women artists for
whom "being found" has often meant being cut off from their
own voice: becoming strangled with another's words.

Rich (1978) continues this motif, with greater power and
surgency, in the poem "Transcendental Etude," in which she
affirms the importance of being rooted in one's own primary
rhythms, one's own self-experience:

The longer I live the more I mistrust
theatricality, the false glamour cast
by performance, the more I know its poverty beside
the truths we are salvaging from
the splitting-open of our lives.
The woman who sits watching, listening,
eyes moving in the darkness
is rehearsing in her body, hearing-out in her blood
a score touched off in her perhaps
by some words, a few chords, from the stage:
a tale only she can tell.

But there are times—perhaps this is one of them—
when we have to take ourselves more seriously or die;
when we have to pull back from the incantations,
rhythms we've moved to thoughtlessly, ...
No one who survives to speak
new language, has avoided this:

the cutting-away of an old force that held her
rooted to an old ground
the pitch of utter loneliness
where she herself and all creation
seem equally dispersed, weightless, her being a cry
to which no echo comes or can ever come

[pp. 74–75].

In this poem, Rich speaks of the dilemma of being born into a world in which we can never be perfectly held or deciphered; in which we yearn for a more perfect mirror to hold us, that only we can hold. And yet, we search until we are forced to give up the illusion of self that has been projected outward and disowned, and stand with our own mirror, turned, to catch whatever facets of the prism might be reflected there:

Vision begins to happen in such a life
as if a woman quietly walked away
from the argument and jargon . . .

[p. 76].

It is then, in the willingness to mourn that which had not been mourned, and to also tolerate the fragments not yet integrated into a tolerable awareness of self and other, that we might sit, in some peace, and contemplate the inevitable. This is the place from which one's own voice might be heard and spoken, as we gather ourselves into our own silence. Without this grounding in our own silence, we too easily lose touch with basic realities of human existence and with our own creativity (Milner, 1987). At that point, life becomes meaningless, a void. In the poem "Merced," Rich (1973) speaks of the treachery we wreak in the world when we allow ourselves to lose our grounding in our selves:

Taking off in a plane
I look down at the city

which meant life to me, not death
and think that somewhere there
a cold center, composed
of pieces of human beings
metabolized, restructured
by a process they do not feel
is spreading in our midst
and taking over our minds
a thing that feels neither guilt
nor rage: that is unable
to hate, therefore to love

[pp. 36–37].

One facet of this grounding is acceptance, an active process for this poet. The willingness to feel gives birth to the ultimate principles to which poets, such as Coleridge (1817), and analysts, such as Bion (1965) and Grotstein (1996), allude. In "From a Survivor," Rich (1973) speaks of the importance of embracing what life has to offer:

and you are wastefully dead
who might have made the leap
we talked, too late, of making

which I live now
not as a leap
but a succession of brief, amazing movements

each one making possible the next

[p. 50].

Our willingness to attune ourselves to our own primary rhythms creates an opening, much like the space offered by silence, which facilitates real being. This is a theme Rich (1989) picks up again, quite powerfully, in "Sleepwalking Next To Death":

Sleep   horns of a snail
               protruding, retracting
What we choose to know
               or not know
                      all these years
sleepwalking
        next to death

                                [p. 17].

In our culture, there tends to be too little appreciation of the nonverbal channels, which leaves our thinking insubstantial and trivialized, cut off as it is from its roots. Whereas Plath's work speaks for what is lost in our failure to make our peace with the language of the body, Rich's work speaks eloquently for the need to reown and reaffirm our roots in culture, history, and the language of material reality: the body and land that grounds it and gives it life. She speaks to the essential unity (O) as represented by the particular manifestations of experience, thereby bringing us back full circle to the source: O. In line with Coleridge, for whom creative thought and self-knowledge were indivisible (Williams and Waddell, 1991), Bion (1965) suggested that reality as such is experienced, not known; ultimately, transformations in O "are related to growth in becoming" (p. 156). Poetry, as exemplified in the works presented here, offers us one form of moving into this realm of becoming, through which we can experience that larger reality we seek, yet never truly obtain, in an ongoing struggle to emerge from this "sleepwalking next to death" (Rich, 1989, p. 17).

EPILOGUE

*I*n spending time sorting through the conceptions contained within this book, I find myself listening in new ways to my patients, as they speak to me from within the realities that constrain their perceptions and preclude further growth or understanding. At times, my attempts to understand where they are stuck fill an important void in their own understanding and the fabric becomes repatterned in ways that offer new meanings and new possibilities. Nowhere has this been more true than in my work with Elena, for whom reality had consisted of a forced choice between her own lack of value and the world's utter hostility. In either case, she had no hope of finding a valued place in a universe in which she had been barred from membership.

A pivotal point in our work together came when I suggested that perhaps what she had interpreted as hatred, hostility, or devaluation might have resulted, rather, from helplessness on the part of the other. This idea became a "selected fact" that reorganized Elena's view of reality. It allowed for a conception of the universe in which people could fail and still have value, and in which people could fail one another and still care. In abeyance was the image of the murderous mother who had destroyed Elena's gifts. Instead, we were confronted with the image of the impotent mother who could find no way to nourish either her daughter or the daughter's gifts.

The tears that Elena had thought were out of reach now came freely—not as guilt, she told me, but as regret. She had not been able to "find" her father before his death, but only in retrospect, as she came to appreciate him as a whole human being, who had loved her but also had failed her. Now, as she thinks about her mother, she marvels: "She didn't hate me. She doesn't shut me off because she doesn't love me. She does love me, she just doesn't know what to do with what I give her, and I keep giving it to her and she keeps shutting it off. I just never got it before. That she has these limits. She isn't an evil monster. And it isn't that she doesn't love me. She just has these limitations."

Through Elena's encounters with my view of her as wholly human, along with my willingness to accept her gifts and her failings, Elena has been able to reconcile these disparate pieces of self and other, rather than resorting to the splitting that had kept human beings incomprehensible to her in spite of her earnest attempts to understand. In a household in which problems in interaction could not be solved, they became taboo. She could neither speak of these interactive failures nor resolve them. Having them at all marked her as inferior, subhuman, and repugnant. Insisting on trying to understand them marked her as incredibly irritating.

When Elena first came into my office, the sessions were marked by her intense efforts to convey "the problem" to me. It was essential that I understand exactly what the problem (Elena) was. As I began to understand Elena, it seemed that the problem was not Elena herself, but rather that she had become so caught between grandiose and debased images of self that she could not find her self. As we have come to understand how Elena's world became patterned, and to thereby break into these conceptualizations and re-image them, there has been a shift in focus. Like a kaleidoscope that has been shaken, we see revealed new, more complex, and infinitely more lovely and intriguing patterns. This was the hope that Elena could not quite believe in: that if she could truly see herself, she would be pleased with what she would encounter.

This is the sleight of hand with which we play with our patients daily. As I told one patient: "It is like we are on a virtual chessboard. From your side, you are terrified of being seen. From my side, I know that your fears are unfounded. You can see that I believe that, but you can't quite believe in my belief sufficiently to come take a look from my side of the board." Herein lies a fundamental challenge of our work: to help our patients to re-vision reality in such a way that they can keep their eyes open sufficiently to make sense of the unique patternings of their experience. Recognizing these patterns helps us to make sense of self and world in ways that encourage mastery and facilitate growth, as we learn to avoid stumbling over the hazards in our paths, and perhaps even to enjoy the encounter.

REFERENCES

Alvarez, A. (1997). Projective identification as a communication: Its grammar in borderline psychotic children. *Psychoanal. Dial.*, 7:753–768.

Angelou, M. (1978). *And Still I Rise.* London: Virago Press.

Anzieu, D. (1979). The sound image of the self. *Internat. Rev. Psycho-Anal.*, 6:23–36.

—— (1984). Fonctions du Moi-Peau. *L'Information Psychiatrique*, 60:869–875.

—— (1993). Autistic phenomena and the skin ego. *Psychoanal. Inq.*, 13:42–48.

Arden, M. (1985). Psychoanalysis and survival. *Internat. J. Psycho-Anal.*, 66:471–480.

Arlow, J. A. (1979). Metaphor and the psychoanalytic situation. *Psychoanal. Quart.*, 48:363–385.

Axelrod, S. G. (1990). *Sylvia Plath: The Wound and the Cure of Words.* Baltimore: Johns Hopkins University Press.

Balint, M. (1953). *Primary Love and Psychoanalytic Technique.* London: Hogarth.

—— (1959). *Thrills and Regressions.* New York: International Universities Press.

Beebe, B. & Lachmann, F. M. (1988). The contributions of mother-infant mutual influence to the origins of self and object representations. *Psychoanal. Psychol.*, 5:305–337.

—— & —— (1994). Representation and internalization in infancy: Three principles of salience. *Psychoanal. Psychol.*, 11:127–165.

—— & —— (1998). Co-constructing inner and relational processes: Self and mutual regulation in infant research and adult treatment. *Psychoanal. Psychol.*, 15:480–516.

—— ——& Jaffe, J. (1997). Mother-infant interaction structures and presymbolic self and object representations. *Psychoanal. Dial.*, 7:133–182.

Bianchedi, E. T. de (1991). Psychic change: The "becoming" of an inquiry. *Internat. J. Psycho-Anal.*, 72:4–15.

Bick, E. (1968). The experience of the skin in early object relations. *Internat. J. Psycho-Anal.*, 49:484–486.

Bion, W. R. (1961). *Experiences in Groups and Other Papers*. London: Routledge.

—— (1962). *Learning from Experience*. London: Heinemann.

—— (1963). *Elements of Psycho-Analysis*. London: Heinemann.

—— (1965). *Transformations*. London: Heinemann.

—— (1967). *Second Thoughts: Selected Papers on Psychoanalysis*. Northvale, NJ: Aronson.

—— (1970). *Attention and Interpretation*. London: Heinemann.

—— (1977). *Seven Servants*. New York: Aronson.

Bohm, D. (1965). The significance of the Minkowski diagram. In: *The Special Theory of Relativity*. New York: W. A. Benjamin, pp. 173–184.

—— (1980). *Wholeness and the Implicate Order*. London: Routledge.

Bohr, N. (1934). The quantum postulate and the recent development of atomic theory. In: *Atomic Physics and Human Knowledge*. Woodbridge, CT: Ox Bow Press, 1987.

—— (1958). Quantum physics and philosophy: Causality and complementarity. In: *Essays 1958–1962 on Atomic Physics and Human Knowledge*. New York: Wiley, pp. 1–7.

Bollas, C. (1987). *The Shadow of the Object: Psychoanalysis of the Unthought Known*. London: Free Association Books.

—— (1992). *Being a Character: Psychoanalysis and Self-Experience*. New York: Hill & Wang.

Bowlby, J. (1973). *Attachment and Loss, Vol. 2*. New York: Basic Books.

Brennan, T. (1997). Social pressure. *Amer. Imago*, 54:257–288.

Breuer, J. & Freud, S. (1893–1895). Studies on hysteria. *Standard Edition*, 2. London: Hogarth Press, 1971.

Briggs, J. & Peat, F. D. (1989). *Turbulent Mirror: An Illustrated Guide to Chaos Theory and the Science of Wholeness*. New York: Harper & Row.

Bromberg, P. M. (1991). On knowing one's patient inside out: The aesthetics of unconscious communication. *Psychoanal. Dial.*, 1:399–422.

Bucci, W. (1997a). Symptoms and symbols: A multiple code theory of somatization. *Psychoanal. Inq.*, 2:151–172.

——(1997b). *Psychoanalysis and Cognitive Science: A Multiple Code Theory.* New York: Guilford.

Charles, M. (1998). On wondering: Creating openings into the analytic space. *J. M. Klein Obj. Rel.*, 16:367–387.

——(1999a). Sibling mysteries: Enactments of unconscious fears and fantasies. *Psychoanal. Rev.*, 86:877–901.

——(1999b). The Piggle: Confrontations with non-existence in childhood. *Internat. J. Psycho-Anal.*, 80:783–795.

——(1999c). The promise of love: A view among women. *Psychoanal. Psychol.*, 16:254–273.

—— (2000a). The intergenerational transmission of unresolved mourning: Personal, familial, and cultural factors. *Samiksa*, 54:65–80.

—— (2000b). Convex and concave, Part 1: Images of emptiness in women. *Amer. J. Psychoanal.*, 60:5–27.

—— (2000c). Convex and concave, Part 2: Images of emptiness in men. *Amer. J. Psychoanal,.* 60:119–138.

——(2001a). A "confusion of tongues": Difficulties in conceptualizing development in psychoanalytic theories. *Kleinian Studies Ejournal:* http://www.human-nature.com/ksej/charles.htm

——(2001b). Stealing beauty: An exploration of maternal narcissism. *Psychoanal. Rev.*, 88:601–622.

——(2001c). Assimilating difference: Traumatic effects of prejudice. *Samiksa*, 55:15–27.

——(2001d). The outsider. *Free Associations*, 8:625–652.

——(2001e). Reflections on creativity: The "intruder" as mystic or Reconciliation with the mother/self. *Free Associations*, 9:119–151.

—— (2002a). Bion's grid: A tool for transformation. *J. Amer. Acad. Psychoanal.*, 30:429–445.

—— (2002b). Creative myth-making: The importance of play. Presented at the annual meeting of the APA Division of Psychoanalysis, New York City, April.

——(in press). Dreamscapes: Portrayals of rectangular spaces in Doris Lessing's *Memoirs of a Survivor* and in dreams. *Psychoanal. Rev.*

—— (forthcoming). Women in psychotherapy on film: Shades of Scarlett Conquering. In: *The Celluloid Couch: Psychoanalysis and Psychotherapy in the Movies*, ed. J. Brandell. Albany, NY: SUNY Press.

Clyman, R. B. (1991). The procedural organization of emotions: A contribution from cognitive science to the psychoanalytic theory of therapeutic action. *J. Amer. Psychoanal. Assn.*, 39(Suppl.):349–382.

Coleridge, S. T. (1817). *Biographia Literaria*, ed. J. Engell & W. J. Bates. London: Routledge & Kegan Paul, 1983.

Concise Oxford Dictionary, 9th ed. (1995). Oxford: Clarendon Press.

Cooper, R. P. & Aslin, R. N. (1994). Developmental differences in infant attention to the spectral properties of infant-directed speech. *Child Dev.*, 65:1663–1667.

Crowther, P. (1993). *Critical Aesthetics and Postmodernism*. Oxford: Clarendon Press.

Denman, C. (1994). Strange attractors and dangerous liaisons: A response to Priel and Schreiber, "On psychoanalysis and non-linear dynamics: The paradigm of bifurcation." *Brit. J. Med. Psychol.*, 67:219–222.

Edkins, W. L. (1997). Symmetry and perceptual and affective development: The analytic object relation. *J. M. Klein Obj. Rel.*, 15:595–610.

Eggum, A. (1978). The theme of death. In: *Edvard Munch: Symbols and Images*. Exhibit catalog. Washington, DC: National Gallery of Art, pp. 143–186.

Eigen, M. (1998). *The Psychoanalytic Mystic*. London: Free Association Books.

Ekman, P. (1982). *Emotion in the Human Face*. Cambridge: Cambridge University Press.

Eliot, T. S. (1943). *On Poetry and Poets*. New York: Farrar, Straus & Giroux.

Erikson, E. H. (1950). *Childhood and Society*. New York: Norton.

Fairbairn, W. R. D. (1952). *Psychoanalytic Studies of the Personality*. London: Routledge.

Fernald, A. (1993). Approval and disapproval: Infant responsiveness to vocal affect in familiar and unfamiliar languages. *Child Dev.*, 64:657–674.

Fogel, A. (1992). Movement and communication in human infancy: The social dynamics of development. *Human Movement Sci.*, 11:387–423.

Fonagy, P. (1998). Moments of change in psychoanalytic theory: Discussion of a new theory of psychic change. *Infant Mental Health J.*, 19:346–353.

————Steele, M., Steele, H., Leigh, T., Kennedy, R., Mattoon, G. & Target, M. (1995). Attachment, the reflective self, and borderline states: The predictive specificity of the Adult Attachment Interview and pathological emotional development. In: *Attachment Research: Social, Developmental, and Clinical Perspectives*, ed. S. Goldberg, R. Muir & J. Kerr. Hillsdale, NJ: The Analytic Press, pp. 233–278.

———— & Target, M. (1997). Attachment and reflective function. *Dev. & Psychopathol.* 9:679–700.

Freud, S. (1900). The interpretation of dreams. *Standard Edition*, 4 & 5. London: Hogarth Press, 1971.

———— (1915). The unconscious. *Standard Edition*, 14:159–215. London: Hogarth Press, 1971.

———— (1921). Group psychology and the analysis of the ego. *Standard Edition*, 18:69–143. London: Hogarth Press, 1971.

———— (1923). The ego and the id. *Standard Edition*, 19:1–66. London: Hogarth Press, 1971.

———— (1925). Negation. *Standard Edition*, 19:235–239. London: Hogarth Press, 1971.

———— (1926). Inhibitions, symptoms and anxiety. *Standard Edition*, 20:87–175. London: Hogarth Press, 1971.

Gaddini, R. (1987). Early care and the roots of internalization. *Internat. Rev. Psycho-Anal.*, 14:321–333.

Gardner, S. (1994). Commentary on Priel and Schreiber, "On psychoanalysis and non-linear dynamics." *Brit. J. Med. Psychol.*, 67:223–225.

Gomberoff, M. J., Noemi, C. C. & De Gomberoff, L. P. (1990). The autistic object: Its relationship with narcissism in the transference and countertransference of neurotic and borderline patients. *Internat. J. Psycho-Anal.*, 71:249–259.

Grotstein, J. S. (1980). A proposed revision of the psychoanalytic concept of primitive mental states: Part 1. Introduction to a newer psychoanalytic metapsychology. *Contemp. Psychoanal.*, 16:479–546.

———— (1985). A proposed revision of the psychoanalytic concept of the death instinct. In: *Yearbook of Psychoanalysis and Psychotherapy*, 1:299–326. Hillsdale, NJ: New Concept Press.

———— (1991). Nothingness, meaninglessness, chaos, and the "black hole" 3: Self- and interactional regulation and the background presence of primary identification. *Contemp. Psychoanal.*, 27:1–33.

———— (1996). Bion's "transformations in 'O'," "the thing-in-itself, and the 'Real'": Toward the concept of the "transcendent position." *J. M. Klein Obj. Rel.*, 14:109–141.

———— (1998). The apprehension of beauty and its relationship to "O." *J. M. Klein Obj. Rel.*, 16:273–284.

———— (2000a). *Who Is the Dreamer Who Dreams the Dream? A Study of Psychic Presences.* Hillsdale, NJ: The Analytic Press.

———(2000b). Inner space. In: *Who Is the Dreamer Who Dreams the Dream? A Study of Psychic Presences*. Hillsdale, NJ: The Analytic Press, pp. 83–99.

———(2000c). The myth of the labyrinth. In: *Who Is the Dreamer Who Dreams the Dream? A Study of Psychic Presences*. Hillsdale, NJ: The Analytic Press, pp. 189–218.

———(2000d). Why Oedipus and not Christ? Part 1. In: *Who Is the Dreamer Who Dreams the Dream? A Study of Psychic Presences*. Hillsdale, NJ: The Analytic Press, pp. 219–253.

Guntrip, H. (1989). *Schizoid Phenomena, Object Relations and the Self*. Madison, CT: International Universities Press.

Hymer, S. (1986). The multidimensional significance of the look. *Psychoanal. Psychol.*, 3:149–157.

Ingold, T. (1990). An anthropologist looks at biology. *Man*, 25:208–229.

Ingram, D. H. (1996). The vigor of metaphor in clinical practice. *Amer. J. Psychoanal.*, 56:17–34.

Innes-Smith, M. (1987). Pre-oedipal identification and the cathexis of autistic objects in the aetiology of adult psychopathology. *Internat. J. Psycho-Anal.*, 68:405–413.

Isaacs, S. (1948). The nature and function of phantasy. *Internat. J. Psycho-Anal.*, 29:73–97.

Jacobs, T. J. (1994). Nonverbal communications: Some reflections on their role in the psychoanalytic process and psychoanalytic education. *J. Amer. Psychoanal. Assn.*, 42:741–762.

Kincanon, E. & Powel, W. (1995). Chaotic analysis in psychology and psychoanalysis. *J. Psychol.*, 129:495–505.

Klein, M. (1930). The importance of symbol-formation in the development of the ego. In: *Love, Guilt and Reparation and Other Works, 1921–1945*. London: Hogarth Press, 1981, pp. 219–232.

———(1946). Notes on some schizoid mechanisms. In: *Envy and Gratitude and Other Works, 1946–1963*. New York: Delacorte, 1975, pp. 1–24.

———(1957). Envy and gratitude. In: *Envy and Gratitude and Other Works, 1946–1963*. New York: Delacorte, 1975, pp. 176–234.

———(1963). On the sense of loneliness. In: *Envy and Gratitude and Other Works, 1946–1963*. New York: Delacorte, 1975, pp. 300–313.

Klein, S. (1980). Autistic phenomena in neurotic patients. *Internat. J. Psycho-Anal.*, 61:395–401.

Knafo, D. (1991). Egon Schiele and Frida Kahlo: The self-portrait as mirror. *J. Amer. Acad. Psychoanal.*, 19:630–647.

—— (1993). *Egon Schiele: A Self in Creation.* London: Associated Universities Press.

Kris, E. (1952). *Psychoanalytic Explorations in Art.* New York: International Universities Press.

Krystal, H. (1966). Giorgio de Chirico: Ego states and artistic production. *Amer. Imago*, 23:210–226.

—— (1988). *Integration and Self-Healing: Affect, Trauma, Alexithymia.* Hillsdale, NJ: The Analytic Press.

Kulka, R. (1997). Quantum selfhood: Commentary on paper by Beebe, Lachmann, and Jaffe. *Psychoanal. Dial.*, 7:183–187.

Kumin, I. (1996). *Pre-Object Relatedness: Early Attachment and the Psychoanalytic Situation.* New York: Guilford.

Lacan, J. (1964). *The Four Fundamental Concepts of Psycho-Analysis.* New York: Norton, 1978.

Lakoff, G. (1987). *Women, Fire, and Dangerous Things.* Chicago: University of Chicago Press.

Langer, S. (1951). *Feeling and Form: A Theory of Art.* New York: Charles Scribner's Sons.

Le Doeuff, M. (1987). Women and philosophy. In: *French Feminist Thought: A Reader*, ed. T. Moi. Oxford: Basil Blackwell, pp. 181–209.

Lessing, D. (1971). Introduction to *The Golden Notebook*, 2nd ed. New York: HarperCollins. Originally published in 1962.

Loeb, D. & Podell, D. (1995). Art and trauma. *Internat. J. Psycho-Anal.*, 76:991–1005.

Machotka, P. (1992). Psychobiography and visual creativity: Four patterns. In: *Emerging Visions of the Aesthetic Process: Psychology, Semiology, and Philosophy*, ed. G. C. Cupchik & J. László. Cambridge: Cambridge University Press, pp. 137–153.

Main, M. (1995). Discourse, prediction and studies in attachment: Implications for psychoanalysis. In: *Research in Psychoanalysis: Process, Development, Outcome*, ed. T. Shapiro & R. N. Emde. Madison, CT: International Universities Press, pp. 209–244.

Mancia, M. (1981). On the beginning of mental life in the foetus. *Internat. J. Psycho-Anal.*, 62:351–357.

Marks, E. & de Courtivron, I., eds. (1981). *New French Feminisms.* New York: Schocken Books.

Matte-Blanco, I. (1959). Expression in symbolic logic of the characteristics of the system Ucs or the logic of the system Ucs. *Internat. J. Psycho-Anal.*, 40:1–5.

—— (1975). *The Unconscious as Infinite Sets: An Essay in Bi-Logic.* London: Duckworth.

—— (1988). *Thinking, Feeling, and Being: Clinical Reflections on the Fundamental Antinomy of Human Beings and World.* London: Routledge.

Maure, G., ed. (1996). *Ana Mendieta.* Barcelona: Ediciones Polígrafa, S.A.

McDougall, J. (1974). Countertransference and primitive communication. In: *Plea for a Measure of Abnormality.* New York: International Universities Press, pp. 247–298.

McLaughlin, J. T. (1993). Nonverbal behaviors in the analytic situation: The search for meaning in nonverbal cues. In: *When the Body Speaks: Psychological Meaning in Kinetic Clues,* ed. S. Kramer & S. Akhtar. Northvale, NJ: Aronson, pp. 131–161.

Meltzer, D. (1975). Adhesive identification. *Contemp. Psychoanal.,* 11:289–310.

Merleau-Ponty, M. (1962). *Phenomenology of Perception,* trans. C. Smith. London: Routledge & Kegan Paul.

—— (1993). Eye and mind. In: *The Merleau-Ponty Aesthetics Reader: Philosophy and Painting,* ed. G. A. Johnson. Evanston, IL: Northwestern University Press, pp. 121–149.

Miall, D. S. (1987). Metaphor and affect: The problem of creative thought. *J. Metaphor & Symbolic Activity,* 2:81–96.

—— & Kuiken, D. (1994). Beyond text theory: Understanding literary response. *Discourse Processes,* 17:337–352.

Milner, M. (1950). *On Not Being Able to Paint.* London: Heinemann, 1957.

—— (1952). The role of illusion in symbol formation. In: *The Suppressed Madness of Sane Men: Forty-four Years of Exploring Psychoanalysis.* London: Tavistock, 1987, pp. 83–113.

—— (1956). Psychoanalysis and art. In: *The Suppressed Madness of Sane Men: Forty-four Years of Exploring Psychoanalysis.* London: Tavistock, 1987, pp. 192–215.

—— (1957). The ordering of chaos. In: *The Suppressed Madness of Sane Men: Forty-four Years of Exploring Psychoanalysis.* London: Tavistock, 1987, pp. 216–233.

———— (1987). *The Suppressed Madness of Sane Men: Forty-four Years of Exploring Psychoanalysis.* London: Tavistock.

Mitrani, J. L. (1995). Toward an understanding of unmentalized experience. *Psychoanal. Quart.*, 64:68–112.

Nicolis, G. & Prigogine, I. (1981). Symmetry breaking and pattern selection in far-from-equilibrium systems. *Proc. Natl. Acad. Sci. USA*, 78:659–663.

Ogden, T. H. (1989). *The Primitive Edge of Experience.* Northvale, NJ: Aronson.

———— (1994). The analytic third: Working with intersubjective clinical facts. *Internat. J. Psycho-Anal.*, 75:3–19.

———— (1995). Analysing forms of aliveness and deadness of the transference-countertransference. *Internat. J. Psycho-Anal.*, 76:695–709.

Opatow, B. (1997). Observation and insight in the science of experience. *Amer. Imago*, 54:289–306.

Oremland, J. D. (1997). *The Origins and Psychodynamics of Creativity: A Psychoanalytic Perspective.* Madison, WI: International Universities Press.

Papousek, M., Bornstein, M. H., Nuzzo, C., Papousek, H. & Symmes, D. (1990). Infant responses to prototypical melodic contours in parental speech. *Infant Behav. & Dev.*, 13:539–545.

Parsons, M. (1988). Suddenly finding it really matters: The paradox of the analyst's non-attachment. *Internat. J. Psycho-Anal.*, 67:475–488.

Penrose, R. (1989). *The Emperor's New Mind: Concerning Computers, Minds and the Laws of Physics.* New York: Oxford University Press.

———— (1994). *Shadows of the Mind: A Search for the Missing Science of Consciousness.* Oxford: Oxford University Press.

Person, E. S. & Klar, H. (1994). Establishing trauma: The difficulty distinguishing between memories and fantasies. *J. Amer. Psychoanal. Assn.*, 42:1055–1081.

Plath, S. (1972). *Winter Trees.* New York: Harper & Row.

Podro, M. (1990). "The landscape thinks itself in me": The comments and procedures of Cézanne. *Internat. Rev. Psycho-Anal.*, 17:401–412.

Poincaré, H. (1952). *Science and Method.* New York: Dover Publications.

Priel, B. & Schreiber, G. (1994). On psychoanalysis and non-linear dynamics: The paradigm of bifurcation. *Brit. J. Med. Psychol.*, 67:209–218.

Quinn, P. C. (1994). The categorization of above and below spatial relations by young infants. *Child Dev.*, 65:58–69.

Rayner, E. (1981). Infinite experiences, affects and the characteristics of the unconscious. *Internat. J. Psycho-Anal.*, 62:403–412.

———(1992). Matching, attunement and the psychoanalytic dialogue. *Internat. J. Psycho-Anal.*, 73:39–54.

Rhode, E. (1998). The enigmatic object: The relation of understanding to being and becoming. *J. M. Klein & Obj. Rel.*, 16:257–272.

Rich, A. (1973). *Diving into the Wreck: Poems 1971–1972*. New York: Norton.

———(1978). *The Dream of a Common Language: Poems 1974–1977*. New York: Norton.

———(1979). *On Lies, Secrets, and Silence: Selected Prose 1966–1978*. New York: Norton.

———(1981). *A Wild Patience Has Taken Me This Far: Poems 1978–1981*. New York: Norton.

———(1984). *The Fact of a Doorframe: Poems Selected and New, 1950–1984*. New York: Norton.

———(1989). *Time's Power: Poems 1985–1988*. New York: Norton.

Rose, G. J. (1980). *The Power of Form: A Psychoanalytic Approach to Aesthetic Form*. New York: International Universities Press.

———(1984). Language and truth: Reflections on Spence's *Narrative Truth and Historical Truth*. *Internat. Forum for Psychoanal.*, 1:19–35.

———(1996). *Necessary Illusion: Art as Witness*. Madison, CT: International Universities Press.

Ryavec, L. S. (1997). Splitting the unconscious: Symmetry, asymmetry, and the principle of the excluded middle. *J. M. Klein Obj. Rel.*, 5:611–630.

———(1998). Rhythms of experience: The interplay of symmetry and asymmetry in development. *Psychoanal. Rev.*, 85:183–196.

Sander, L. (1985). Toward a logic of organization in psycho-biological development. In: *Biologic Response Styles: Clinical Implications*. Washington DC: American Psychiatric Press, pp. 20–36.

Sandler, J. (1976). Countertransference and role-responsiveness. *Internat. Rev. Psycho-Anal.*, 3:43–47.

Schacter, D. L. (1992). Understanding implicit memory: A cognitive neuroscience approach. *Amer. Psychol.*, 47:559–569.

Schore, A. N. (1994). *Affect Regulation and the Origin of the Self: The Neurobiology of Emotional Development*. Hillsdale, NJ: Lawrence Erlbaum Associates.

Segal, H. (1957). Notes on symbol formation. *Internat. J. Psycho-Anal.*, 38:391–397.

—— (1981). *The Work of Hanna Segal: A Kleinian Approach to Clinical Practice*. New York: Aronson.

Seligman, S. (1998). Child psychoanalysis, adult psychoanalysis, and developmental psychology: Introduction to symposium on child analysis, part 2. *Psychoanal. Dial.*, 9:79–86.

—— (1999). Integrating Kleinian theory and intersubjective infant research: Observing projective identification. *Psychoanal. Dial.*, 9:129–159.

Sexton, A. (1988). *Selected Poems of Anne Sexton*. Boston: Houghton Mifflin.

Shabad, P. (1993), Repetition and incomplete mourning: The intergenerational transmission of traumatic themes. *Psychoanal. Psychol.*, 10:61–75.

Shklovsky, V. (1917). Art as technique. In: *Russian Formalist Criticism: Four Essays*, ed. & trans. L. T. Lemon & M. J. Reis. Lincoln: University of Nebraska Press, 1965.

Smith, H. F. (1990). Cues: The perceptual edge of the transference. *Internat. J. Psycho-Anal.*, 71:219–228.

Spinoza, B. (1677). *Ethics: The Collected Works of Spinoza*, ed. & trans. E. Curley. Princeton, NJ: Princeton University Press.

Stang, N. (1972). *Edvard Munch*. Oslo: Johan Grundt Tanum Forlag.

Steinberg, S. & Weiss, J. (1954). The art of Edvard Munch and its function in his mental life. *Psychoanal. Quart.*, 23:409–423.

Stern, D. N. (1985). *The Interpersonal World of the Infant: A View from Psychoanalysis and Developmental Psychology*. New York: Basic Books.

—— Sander, L. W., Nahum, J. P., Harrison, A. M., Lyons-Ruth, K., Morgan, A. C., Bruschweiler-Stern, N. & Tronick, E. Z. (1998). Non-interpretive mechanisms in psychoanalytic therapy: The "something more" than interpretation. *Internat. J. Psycho-Anal.*, 79:903–921.

Symington, J. (1985). The survival function of primitive omnipotence. *Internat. J. Psycho-Anal.*, 66:481–487.

Symington, N. (1983). The analyst's act of freedom as agent of therapeutic change. *Internat. Rev. Psycho-Anal.*, 10:283–291.

Target, M. & Fonagy, P. (1996) Playing with reality: 2. The development of psychic reality from a theoretical perspective. *Internat. J. Psycho-Anal.*, 77:459–479.

Tomkins, S. S. (1962). *Affect, Imagery, Consciousness: Volume 1: The Positive Affects.* New York: Springer.

————(1982). Affect theory. In: *Emotion in the Human Face,* ed. P. Ekman. Cambridge: Cambridge University Press, pp. 353–395.

————(1987). Script theory. In: *The Emergence of Personality,* ed. J. Aronoff, A. I. Rabin & R. A. Zucker. New York: Springer, pp. 147–216.

Trevarthen, C. (1989). Development of early social interactions and their effective regulation of human growth. In: *Neurobiology of Early Infant Behaviour,* ed. C. von Euler, H. Forssberg & H. Lagerkrantz. New York: Macmillan, pp. 191–216.

————(1995). Mother and baby—Seeing artfully eye to eye. In: *The Artful Eye,* ed. R. Gregory, J. Harris, P. Heard & D. Rose. Oxford: Oxford University Press, pp. 157–200.

Tronick, E. (1989). Emotions and emotional communication in infants. *Amer. Psychol.,* 44:112–119.

————Bruschweiler-Stern, N., Harrison, A. M., Lyons-Ruth, K., Morgan, A. C., Nahum, J. P., Sander, L. W. & Stern, D. N. (1998). Dyadically expanded states of consciousness and the process of therapeutic change. *Infant Mental Health J.,* 19:290–299.

Tustin, F. (1969). Autistic processes. *J. Child Psychother.,* 2:23–39.

————(1984). Autistic shapes. *Internat. Rev. Psycho-Anal.,* 11:279–290.

————(1986). *Autistic Barriers in Neurotic Patients.* New Haven: Yale University Press.

————(1991). Revised understandings of psychogenic autism. *Internat. J. Psycho-Anal.,* 72:585–591.

Vigée-Lebrun, E. (1903). *Memoirs of Madame Vigée-Lebrun,* trans. L. Strachey. New York: Doubleday, Page.

Williams, M. H. & Waddell, M. (1991). *The Chamber of Maiden Thought: Literary Origins of the Psychoanalytic Model of the Mind.* London: Tavistock/Routledge.

Winnicott, D. W. (1953). Transitional objects and transitional phenomena: A study of the first not-me possession. *Internat. J. Psycho-Anal.,* 34:89–97.

————(1960). Ego distortion in terms of true and false self. In: *The Maturational Processes and the Facilitating Environment.* New York: International Universities Press, 1965, pp. 140–152.

————(1963). Communicating and not communicating leading to a study of certain opposites. In: *The Maturational Processes and the*

Facilitating Environment. New York: International Universities Press, 1965, pp. 179–192.

——— (1965). *The Maturational Processes and the Facilitating Environment.* New York: International Universities Press.

——— (1971). *Playing and Reality.* London: Routledge.

——— (1974). Fear of breakdown. *Internat. Rev. Psycho-Anal.*, 1:103–107.

——— (1977). *The Piggle: An Account of the Psychoanalytic Treatment of a Little Girl.* New York: International Universities Press.

Zerbe, K. J. (1987). Mother and child: A psychobiological portrait of Mary Cassatt. *Psychoanal. Rev.*, 74:45–61.

Zuckerandl, V. (1956). *Sound and Symbol.* Princeton, NJ: Princeton University Press.

INDEX

179